THE APPARITIONS OF ABBEVILLE

THE
APPARITIONS
of ABBEVILLE

The History & Mystery of
the South Carolina Lakelands

MARJORIE LANELLE

Palmetto Publishing Group
Charleston, SC

The Apparitions of Abbeville
Copyright © 2018 by Marjorie LaNelle
All rights reserved

First Edition

Printed in the United States

ISBN-13: 978-1-64111-166-9
ISBN-10: 1-64111-166-6

Dedication

I would like to dedicate this book to my siblings: my big brother, Stacey Lamar Chrisley, whose phenomenal photography is featured in this book; and to my sweet baby sister, Karen LeAnne Chrisley-Roller, to whom I look up. Though we all may not agree with one another all the time (especially on the topic of ghosts), you have both always supported me and loved me for who I am. For this, I thank you. I love you both and am blessed that God chose you two to be the ones who call me: "sister."

Also, to Elaine Rhodes and Deidre Parks, two of my best friends, I dedicate this book, and I sincerely thank you both for always being by my side, supporting my writing, but most of all for your prayers of protection.

To Joann Bonds Hughes (my "other mother") and Mary Jo Tolbert (my godmother), thank you for being so supportive in every aspect of my life. I have learned much from the both of you, and I value your advice, insight, love, and friendship!

I love you all.

BOO!

Table of Contents

Introduction

AMONG THE VARIOUS PLACES WHERE SPIRITS MAY roam, Abbeville, South Carolina, is believed by many to be one of *the* most haunted towns in the southeastern United States. As you read the pages ahead, you will begin to understand why this quiet little Southern town is believed to be so spiritually active.

"There's hardly a corner or street in this town that *doesn't* have a ghost story of some sort," stated local business owner and longtime resident Judson Arce. "Abbeville has so much history that it is impossible *not* to have such intriguing stories."

I intended for this book to be less than sixty-five pages, as it began merely as a tourism project, but it ended up being so much more—and almost over twice as long as anticipated. Hauntingly eerie stories kept pouring in. This book was scheduled to be published in 2017, but there were just too many stories that I could not possibly leave out. It was either include them all in one book or possibly have a second volume, but I *could not* leave any of these stories out.

Ghostly accounts in this book range from local folk-lore to family ghost stories that have been told for decades, passed down from generation to generation. Others are from personal experiences as told by common folk, story-tellers, and the author herself.

To say the least, Abbeville is surely one of the most haunted cities one may choose to visit—if not *the* most haunted city!

So now, as always, it is time to ponder this question: Do *you* believe in ghosts?

Sit back and relax as Marjorie LaNelle introduces you to *The Apparitions of Abbeville.*

CHAPTER 1
A Little Bit of History

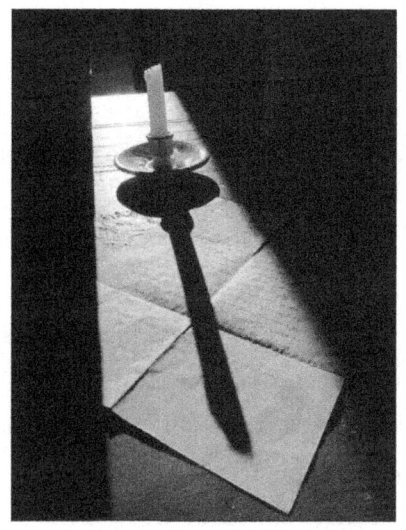

A HUGUENOT SETTLER, ONE OF ABBEVILLE, SOUTH Carolina's founding fathers, was Dr. John de la Howe. He named this beautiful piece of land after his hometown, Abbeville, France. It is believed that de la Howe also initiated the idea of designing Abbeville's city square. Made up of older buildings, the square seems to be the heart of

Abbeville and is deemed so appropriately, as it is located in the center of town. The majority of these buildings have served and still serve in a commercial capacity. Most structures in and around the square were designed and built in the late nineteenth and early twentieth centuries. However, three large fires in the latter part of the 1800s claimed many of the original buildings and destroyed most of the town's historical records. The rebuilding and reconstruction of this area still forms a square and is, too, how Abbeville is seen and viewed today. The brick-paved roads that meander within and around the square are still quite lovely and easy to travel, no matter the mode of transportation.

Majestic cathedrals, historic homes of all sizes and shapes, and beautiful, enchanting architecture are among the features that attract tourists and visitors alike to this quaint Southern town.

Massive oak trees stand tall and proud as if to welcome everyone who enters the historic square in the center of town. The friendliness of the residents is quite obvious and seems most sincere. The ambiance is that of true Southern hospitality, and depending upon the season, the smell of honeysuckle, gardenias, magnolias, daffodils, and roses lingers in the air. *This*, folks, is Abbeville, South Carolina.

Mix into that lovely recipe a heap of history, a dash of mystery, and a pinch of nostalgia, and you get one of the most beautiful and intriguing cities in the nation.

Natives to this area were the Cherokee Indians. Later came Patrick Calhoun with a group of Scots-Irish settlers (eighteenth century), and then the Huguenots, so one may genuinely greet you with several different types of hellos: "A-ho"; "Bonjour!"; or "Top of the mornin' to ya!" However, being in the present-day South, you are most likely to simply get a friendly "Hey!" or if you are in a group of people, you'll probably get a very welcoming and energetic "Hey, y'all!"—most often accompanied by a genuine smile, hand wave, or, if close enough to your greeter, firm handshake or hug. No matter how you are welcomed, it is most likely that if you arrive as a stranger, you will leave as not just an acquaintance, but a friend.

Among the famous sons of Abbeville (and there are many), Revolutionary War hero General Andrew Pickens called Abbeville home. From 1765 to 1787, Pickens owned much of the land, and on that land flowed what is known as the Big Spring, which is still marked today, located behind the current courthouse. This freshwater spring was a major water source for everyone in Abbeville, and Pickens generously donated the spring to the residents of Abbeville as a public water source. The town square was built up near this spring and, well, over several decades, the spring ran dry. Below is a photo of the famously known spring.

Pickens also had a very successful trading post on which he later built a safe haven for the people of Abbeville to protect them against native "Indian attacks." It is said that Pickens even built a house with a trapdoor where people could have access to the spring or hide if they were to be attacked.

Abbeville was not only very instrumental in the Revolutionary War, but also in the Civil War (other names for which include "The War Between the States" and "The War of Northern Aggression," depending on who you ask). Many people refer to Abbeville as the "Birthplace and Deathbed of the Confederacy." The Birthplace of the Confederacy refers to an event that took place on November 22, 1860. Over three thousand people gathered in an area referred to as Secession Hill (located behind the present-day courthouse). Passionate secession speeches fueled the fire of the Civil War, and just weeks later, a full-fledged war ensued. Today, Secession Hill is marked as a historical landmark and is located on the appropriately named Secession Avenue.

The title "Deathbed of the Confederacy" was earned just a few blocks over from Secession Hill, at the Burt-Stark Mansion. On May 5, 1865, the president of the Confederacy, Jefferson Davis, signed the papers to dissolve the Confederacy in the front parlor of this historic home.

At that time, rumors spread about what some refer to as the "Confederate gold" (treasure). It was said to be lost, hidden, or stolen during the few days and weeks before and after the dissolution. Rumors and folklore of such "gold" suggest that the treasure may somewhere be hidden in Abbeville. Others believe that the money was split between those who dissolved the conflict and they went their own separate ways, setting their families up for several generations. Yet there are still some who say that this so-called treasure never existed. Explorers, and those whose curiosity has gotten the better of them, have dived in nearby bodies of water and in bodies of water wherein President Jefferson spent time, believing the treasure was tossed overboard for safekeeping and hidden until it may one day be retrieved. In any case, to this day, no Confederate gold has surfaced or been found in either of these scenarios. The legend of the Confederate gold remains one of the biggest mysteries in Abbeville and, from time to time, a great conversation topic.

This brings to mind the infamous tunnels that run beneath several homes and within and around the square in the downtown area of Abbeville—but that is another story for another time.

Residents of Abbeville call it a city, while others simply refer to it as a town. Either way, many good people call it home.

CHAPTER 2

Bernibrooks Inn

WILLIAM BROOKS BUILT HIS DAUGHTER MAGGIE Whitfield Brooks her very own home in 1860. The simple and practical yet very large house was located right beside his home and was constructed in the Colonial Revival design.

Mr. Brooks hoped that Maggie would someday marry and have a large family, and this house would surely have been more than sufficient. Sadly, this dream never became reality. Maggie Brooks never married or had any children.

Instead, the very content young woman transformed the dream home into a boarding house. Traveling railroad workers utilized this haven often. It was clean, convenient, and affordable for such travelers as the economy was being rebuilt after the Civil War.

Miss Brooks took care of many guests during her lifetime and died at the age of eighty-seven, never having moved from her home. As for the house, the next fifty years were not kind. Natural elements, weather, and time took its toll on the once beautiful yet humble abode. The Brooks house that was once a home fell into disrepair. At that time, an elderly couple by the last name of Nichols owned the home. They were unable to keep the structure sound and intact; therefore, it was deemed unlivable. A family by the name of Parnell then purchased the property but never fully restored it.

Then, in 1993, Maggie Brooks's home was lovingly purchased by the present-day owners, the Berni family. Little did they know that when they started the renovations they would bring more than the house back to life! Mysteriously, as the new owners explained it, a single penny was found near the top of the front room stairway. As renovations continued, pennies were continuously found all over the property, in and outside of the house. It could have been assumed that someone collected pennies, but later, the Bernis would discover the true significance of those little copper coins.

After ten years, a large monetary investment, and hundreds of long hours of hard work, the Bernibrooks Inn had its grand opening as a bed and breakfast in 2003; the house would once again be open to cater to the needs of visitors, tourists, and tired travelers! All guests were again welcomed in, and the lady of the house would treat them as family. Southern hospitality is at its best still today, just as it was back then. The presence of Maggie Brooks has reportedly been seen and sensed on numerous occasions, and she is surely pleased to see that her legacy of caring for others is being carried on.

Adjacent to the inn sits the home of Maggie's sister, which their father is also credited as having built. The sister reportedly married, but to the family's dismay, her husband was rumored to be a very harsh man and had even been accused of murder. Over the years, there have been many tales told about both the "sister houses," but there is one story that is shared more than any of the others. This is the story of a traveling soldier that Maggie Brooks took in and cared for. His name was Carter Bridwell, and what follows is his story.

A PENNY FOR YOUR THOUGHTS?

My name is Carter C. Bridwell, and I proudly served in the Confederate Army. Imagine, if you will, the South in the mid- to late-1800s: piles of ashy residue from burned plantations; wounded and dead soldiers along the roadside; poor, misplaced families; and most disturbingly, dirty and hungry orphaned children. The stench of death, I remember, was always in the air. That's what I witnessed during the battle between the States—things that neither my mind nor my heart, as a matter of fact, would ever be able to erase. These memories were forever embedded, not just in my mind, but in my dreams, my thoughts, my very being. My soul.

The year was 1868. The war was finally over. I had been able to make contact with my family through letters to let them know I was alive. I was very weak and frail and was in the state of Virginia at the time, which is where my last assigned army post was. Yes, I was alive, but very weak and frail. I needed money and strength to get home. Oh, I had plenty of money that my family had sent to me—bless their hearts, they meant well—but the money was Confederate money, and at this point, it was useless! I even had an owner of a general store laugh at me and say that the only thing my money was good for was to use as kindling to start a fire, which I often thought of doing in the cold mountains of Virginia at night. But instead, I just held on, walking toward home, as many steps as I could, day by day. I knew that if I had made it through the war alive, my determination would hopefully, somehow, get me back home to the state of Georgia.

Every day I walked alongside the railroad beds that led toward home. I had tried on more than one occasion to pay the railroad conductor to let me ride the train. Each time the answer was no. Again, my money was of no value to them. There were many times that I would hear the rumbling of the train on the tracks, and as the thundering sound grew closer, I thought about just lying down across the tracks and ending it all. But each time I had that thought, all I could see in my mind was my mama running out of her house, screen door slamming, with her arms open wide and tears in her eyes, to welcome me home from the war. At one point, I thought I even smelled her freshly baked biscuits. My mouth watered. As this train passed and its whistle blew loudly, black smoke flew into the air. This reminded me that my daddy was home waiting as well, poking the fire in the woodstove, keeping our humble home warm. I just couldn't give up. I was hungry and ever so tired. I could feel my ribs through my heavy coat as I lay down for the night underneath a large oak tree. Hopefully I would dream of Mama's cooking and not the war. Each night I fell asleep, I was not sure whether I would wake up in the same spot or wake up in "glory." That's what Mama called heaven.

The next day, as the sun began to rise, a few of my fellow soldiers came walking along the way, each going to a different state to get back home. They, too, were weak and on their own missions—to get back to their loved ones. So, after a few miles, we again parted ways, each in a different direction.

Within the next two days, I had grown even more sickly, tired, and nearly lame. I wasn't sure if my lips were parched, chapped, or both. But they hurt, and they were peeling. I could taste blood on them. With the elements taking a toll on me, I was at the point where I was beginning to doubt if I would ever see my mother or father again. I wasn't sure if my body could endure yet another sunrise. The vision of my mother's embrace played over and over in my mind as I imagined how she would run to me when I finally made it home. Oh, the yearning I had to be in my own bed! Sheets and a pillow, that's what I missed most at nighttime, and never again would I complain about chopping wood for the fireplace, stove, or heater! I had to press on. My will and faith kept my feet moving.

I was no longer in Virginia, and I had passed through North Carolina. I had to be somewhere in South Carolina. That was the last thought I remember. I must have lost consciousness. I don't remember falling asleep, but when I was awakened by the sound of a train whistle, my supply bag was missing, as was most all my Confederate money. Everything had been taken except for the clothes on my back. The only money I had left was the money in my army-issued wool sock—several worthless paper bills and a few coins rolled up in those bills.

I could hear faint piano music and the sounds of a blacksmith pinging on some iron. There was a town close by! I was so weary that I was not sure if it was North Carolina or South Carolina, but it felt friendly to me. Little did I know that this little city would show me so much needed compassion and hospitality; I could feel it. I was on friendly ground! As I made my way from the train depot, I walked up a small hill. The town was in sight. I learned by reading the depot sign that I was in Abbeville, South Carolina.

As I made my way toward the town with my tattered and beaten boots, I approached the town square. It was a welcomed sight, and thankfully, civilization I had not seen for miles and miles, and for days and days on end. I found my way to the blacksmith near the livery stable. I asked him about somewhere to rest, get cleaned up and possibly a hot meal. He pointed me to a house about an eighth of a mile away. He said there was a woman named Maggie there who had a boarding house. He again pointed me in her direction, and when I finally made it to her home, she was more than willing to take me in. She even accepted just a portion of my worthless money as payment. Tears filled my eyes. I was over halfway home.

Over the next several months, she nursed me back to health and I was able to regain my strength. If ever there was an angel in human form, this woman was indeed one!

We had many long conversations over morning coffee and evening tea. We talked about the world, we talked about God, and we talked about anything and everything, just never about the war. Sometimes Maggie would catch me staring out the window or even staring at the ceiling. She would always break my stare by asking, "A penny for your thoughts?" To which I would respond, "You know that Lincoln is on the penny and I don't like him!" Then we would both laugh. It was her way to be my saving grace from the silence and horrific scenes that ran through my mind from the war.

Maggie usually boarded rooms to railroad workers and didn't have to serve as a personal nurse, but she took me in and cared for me as if I were a member of her own family. She catered to my every need, and always before any of the other guests, but, mind you, she never neglected anyone. She would one day be the perfect wife for a very lucky man.

I was able to write to my family more often and keep in touch with them on a regular basis now. For the months that I was under Maggie's care, my family had saved up some good money and sent it to me. I was now more than able to find my way home; I might even have enough new money to ride the train home! And even though a grown adult, I was still yearning to see my mother's worry-stricken face when her son finally made it home from the war.

Well, the day finally came when I had to leave Miss Maggie's boarding house, not knowing if I would ever return. As I made the last payment on my room that had not only become my temporary home but my safe haven for so many months, I saw a look in Maggie's eyes that I had never noticed before. As our hands touched when I gave her the money, her eyes spoke to me as her words never had. We gazed into each other's eyes as we had never done before. This stare was so different from the others. I wanted to hold her, but my heart was still yearning for home. "A penny for your thoughts?" I asked her. She was beautiful, and I had never noticed just how beautiful until this moment. The front door opened, and a traveler came in looking for a room.

"We just had one open up." Maggie smiled. "Put your suitcase over by the staircase, and I will get you signed in."

I turned and ran up the staircase to gather my hat and coat. As I reached to close the door to my room, I took one last look and turned to head home. I stood at the top of the staircase for the last time. I jingled the change in my pocket, thankful that I now had money to get home. There must have been a small hole in my pocket because a penny dropped and landed on a step near the top of the stairs. As I reached down to pick it up, I decided to leave it for Miss Maggie. This was to show her my gratitude for all she had done and a way for her to always remember me. This young Southern lady had literally saved my life. Yes, my life was worth so much more than just a penny, and so was the compassion and care she had so generously shown to me. But we had grown to know each other so well that she would know my intentions were of good nature. Maggie would know that this penny would mean I would never forget her, and I hoped she would never forget me.

I left the penny near the top of the stairs, turning the penny, of course, intentionally facedown as to protest that Lincoln's face was on it, as I was opposed to every tactic and view of his. I smiled as I whispered, "A penny for your thoughts?" and descended the stairs. I left that day with no further goodbye. I closed the door behind me as Maggie was checking in her next guests. I knew if I turned around for another goodbye, I might never leave. I felt in my heart that one day I would return.

It is believed by many that Maggie was quite smitten with the handsome young soldier. She never married anyone else because of her love for Carter. She never moved from the home and died an old maid. Apparently, her hopes were for Carter to return to her; he never did. She never even knew if he made it home to Georgia. He never wrote to her or contacted her in any way.

For years, Maggie would be out and about town, or sometimes in church or other places, and she would hear a gentleman rattle the change in his pocket. Each time, she would excitedly turn to see if it was Carter. Sadly, it was not. Throughout her life, she would hear whispers of Carter asking, "Penny for your thoughts?" only to then realize it was her imagination.

Many visitors and guests are convinced that they have seen a transparent woman walking through the house, or a woman in period clothing peering out of the front door window as if waiting on someone to arrive.

Other accounts are of a male presence walking up closely behind female guests in the house. He then gently whispers, "Penny for your thoughts?"—and disappears.

Please note, as per Karen Berni, current owner of the haunted bed and breakfast: "On the sixty-eighth day of each year, the spirit of Carter C. Bridwell can be heard jingling coins in his pocket. Some have even said that they have seen his apparition at the top of the stairs, and even in the room where Maggie nursed him back to health. The year that Carter made his way to Maggie was 1868, and that happened to be a leap year, so the sixty-eighth day of the year then was March 8. On regular calendar years, March 9 is the day to await Carter's spirit at the Bernibrooks Inn. To this day, pennies are mysteriously found all around the house and property. When we were renovating the house, a penny unexpectedly appeared near the top of the stairs and I permanently affixed it to a step near the top of the staircase. It was, of course, glued facedown, just like Carter would have left it—with Lincoln facing down."

The Bernibrooks Inn is located at 200 West Pinckney Street in Abbeville, South Carolina, and is still an active bed and breakfast. The Bernis welcome and invite everyone to visit their reputedly haunted historical home.

In conclusion, Mrs. Berni added, "Come, stay, and see the penny at the top of the stairs!"

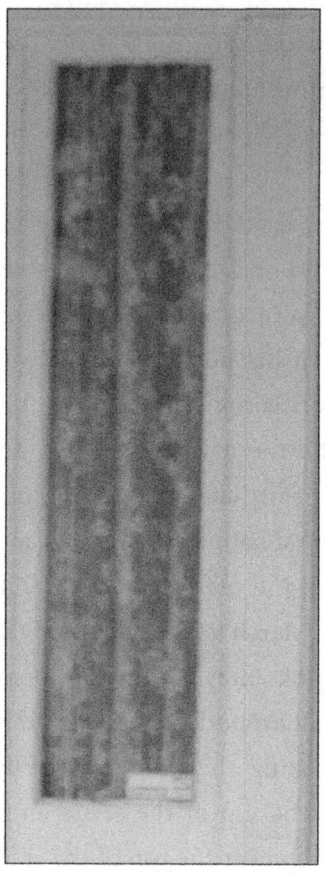

What do you see in the top left-hand corner of this photo? Could it be the face of Miss Maggie Brooks waiting for her long-lost love to return? A penny for your thoughts?

CHAPTER 3

The General's House

Located at 211 North Main Street, this colorful and spooky home served for decades as a private residence but now serves as a museum. With its magnificent architecture and unique features, it is most commonly referred to as the "McGowan House." Believed by many to be haunted, this masterpiece is most mysterious.

Titled on the historic registry as the McGowan-Barksdale-Bundy House, the last owner, J.D. Bundy, deeded this beautifully intriguing Queen-Anne-style house to the Abbeville County Historical Society in 1989. The society from then until present day calls this house their home and holds meetings and events there as well as offering tours of the historic landmark.

This property has also earned the nickname the "General's House," as two of the former owners and residents were generals, Confederate Brigadier General Samuel McGowan and WWII General William E. Barksdale, who was the last owner to actually dwell in the house with his family.

General Samuel McGowan, who had this beautiful masterpiece of a home built, was not only a general, but a lawyer and a jurist. In 1841, McGowan moved from his hometown of Laurens, South Carolina, to Abbeville, where he purchased a Gothic Revival home from the widow of Lieutenant Colonel James M. Perrin, CSA (who was killed at the battle of Chancellorsville during the Civil War). That particular home burned in 1887, and upon the same foundation, McGowan had this magnificent structure built.

Designed and built in 1888 by Atlanta architect G.L. Norman, the breathtaking towers, turrets, and multifaceted roof capture the attention of most all who pass. Other facets that make this home unique include the use of various textures in the materials on the exterior and the obvious talent of the architect who utilized different shapes and sizes for the home's windows. There is even a multicolored interior window located over a landing on the stairwell that when the sun shines into the home and the window is positioned properly, the figure of a colorful cross can be seen. Built-in furniture and pocketed windows and doors are also features that were ahead of their time when the house was constructed.

There are eight rooms in the basement that were once used for several different domestic activities, where various chores were carried out. There is also a separate root cellar that is hidden below the majestic home.

The second floor, which is the main floor, was utilized for entertainment and reading. This level consists of four main rooms: a library, a parlor, a large living hall, and a kitchen/dining area.

On the third floor, accessible by a grand staircase, is a central hall that led into four separate, rather large bedrooms.

The top level of the home is where the commodious attic is located.

As in most homes built in the late 1800s and early 1900s, there are many secret hidden areas within the house. It was also rumored that the secret tunnels in Abbeville may have been, at one time, accessible underneath the house.

There are a few pet grave markers on the property that many mistake as human headstones, but they are not.

In recent years, a train caboose and three servant cabins were added to the property, all of which have significant historical value in their own right. A military museum is also housed inside the home.

Now that you know some of this house's history, you can read about a little mystery that dwells within these walls. Here are a few examples of the most recently reported ghostly happenings at the McGowan's House, as told by a local, anonymous reporter and photographer.

THE GHOSTLY TOUR

It was an early spring day, and the glistening morning dew lay upon the lush, green grass. My friend and I were on a mission: We were going to photograph the outside of the beautiful, colorful, yet weathered McGowan house in Abbeville. Passing by the church next door, we parked in the back of the castle-like structure of a house, where there was a dirt and gravel driveway. There was still a slight chill in the air as we both climbed out of my car. Dressed very casually in our jeans and sweatshirts, we were excited and on our way. We had both always admired this home from a distance, and it looked especially creepy at night. By now, our sneakers were dampened by the wet grass, as it was a pretty good distance from the driveway to the house. We shot a few photos of the back of the intriguing home and then made our way around to the front of the home. Just looking up at the massive structure and seeing morning fog around our ankles sent chills up and down my spine. I felt as if I were in a horror movie. Even though we were alone, I felt as if we were being watched and followed by unseen forces. We were definitely *not* alone.

As we walked up onto the large, wooden front porch of the massive three-story home, each step creaked beneath our feet. We made it onto the porch and sat down on the damp, wooden rocking chairs that adorned the entrance of the home. We began to wipe off the freshly cut grass that clung to our sneakers with the dew. I caught a whiff of fresh blooming flowers as the wind blew ever so softly between the two of us. I closed my eyes to enjoy the fresh morning ambiance and pretended I was at a castle. My daydreaming was interrupted by my friend announcing that the front door was open as she stepped inside. I told her we needed to knock, ring a doorbell, or at least call out to someone to make sure we were allowed to enter. Of course, she ignored me. But before she even got three steps into the entryway, we were greeted by a very nice older gentleman. He seemed to come out of nowhere, very quietly, almost like a ninja. I honestly have no idea where he came from.

He explained that he was there as an overseer to the property. He spoke in almost a whisper, and his smile was friendly but odd in a creepy kind of way. Something just seemed off. My friend continued to bounce right on into the house, oblivious to anything the man was telling us. His wrinkled face seemed to be trusting, but I noticed that his brown eyes seemed to be so dark I couldn't even see a pupil, and he only had a few random eyelashes. His eyebrows were all gray and long—long hairs that went in every direction. One could have brushed them with a comb, they were so wiry and long. I then noticed the age spots on his hands as his hand reached out to shake mine. His hands were so very rough. I could tell he'd never been afraid of hard work throughout his long life. By now, my friend was shooting away with her camera, seemingly still unaware of anything but her own agenda.

"Y'all come on in," he said as he carefully closed the front door and locked it behind me. "We get a lot of people who slow down to look at the house from the outside as they drive by." He stopped and turned to smile again over his aged and slightly hunched back and added, "But it seems that nobody stops like y'all did to come in to see the inside of the house. It's like they are all scared of the house." It took him a few slow steps to get in front of my friend and me. It was obvious that he was going to be our tour guide whether we liked it or not. "Usually they want me to take people's money to show them the house, but I ain't gonna do that to y'all," he said as he reached for his cane at the bottom of the first landing of the massive, intricate staircase. I thanked him for the free tour. "Y'all can take all the pictures you want, but don't be surprised what you catch on your film," he said as he cackled and gave an eerie chuckle.

"What did you say your name was?" I asked as we followed him slowly toward the middle of the house.

"I didn't," he responded without missing a beat. With no further explanation, he *never* told me his name, and I dared not ask again. We just kept walking, shooting photos, and following the crooked little frail man.

The very first area of the house that we started in was, of course, the basement. It seemed like it took us forever to get there, but we did not rush him. All I kept thinking was that this old man was somehow going to kill us right then and there, on the spot, and bury us underneath the house. No one would ever find us because no one even knew we were going there that day! My imagination really does get out of hand sometimes. Besides, I know I am not a small person, but I was sure I could outrun him, and I was sure he couldn't kill me with his cane, as there was no way he could muster up the energy, strength, or momentum to swing it at me and hit me without him falling down and breaking a hip. I decided in my own mind that I would call him "George"—yes, George it was! "Hey, George," I said with my inside voice. "How are you?" I then silently giggled to myself at my own thoughts. I am in need of therapy, yes, I know, but today wasn't the day for that! I was determined to make the best of this creepy situation and get some good pictures.

On my own accord, I was making light of the situation while my friend was just bouncing around as usual as if

this were all normal and okay. She had no fear at all. But...
neither did she see the things that I saw that day.

We were finally in the basement area.

George explained to us that the basement was made up
of eight rooms, one of which particularly caught my attention. It was on the right side facing the house, where I would I
have described as being directly underneath the "gentlemen's
room" (above us on the main floor). It was a rather large
area. It smelled like dirt—clean, swept, light, and sandy dirt.
I closed my eyes for a moment, and I felt as if I were taken
back in time. I could see a lovely Caucasian lady with her hair
up in a neatly groomed bun, with whispers of hair encom-
passing her simple, naturally beautiful face. She was dressed
modestly with a high-neck lace blouse that buttoned in the
front and at each wrist. An oval cameo broach was vertically
pinned directly in the center of the neck of her lace-trimmed
blouse. Her long black skirt was that of the late 1800s and
matched her raven hair. A wide belt was tied around her
tiny waist. She appeared to be teaching, as she was holding a
book. I found myself not only back in time, but apparently, I
was in a makeshift schoolroom. There were several children
there, all, including the teacher, oblivious to my presence.
The children were Caucasian, Native American, and African-
American. Each sat on a makeshift chair that was simply a
tree stump stool. Each child had a rectangular chalkboard
that rested upon their knees, and each had their own piece of
chalk. They were learning to read and write. Only the white

children were wearing shoes. The others' feet, I noticed, were bare and rather dirty.

Suddenly, I was startled, and my concentration was broken when my friend called my name. I was then back in the present day. I looked around the room and no longer saw the image that was once before me. All I saw was the dirt floor and the open sides of the basement with bricks scattered around.

Our tour guide was ready to move on, and I was now more than curious about what I had just experienced. George looked at me again, but this time it was with a tilt of his head and with one eye closed in a wink, almost like he knew I had experienced or seen something odd. When I questioned him about the area we had just left, he sternly said it didn't matter. A few steps farther he stopped and, without even looking at either one of us, began to explain in his raspy voice, "A long time ago, only white children could be taught to read and write—not any other kids, just the white ones. I heard there used to be a young woman to teach all the children to read and write. It didn't matter what they looked like, but she had to do it in secret, so she taught 'em down here in the basement so nobody would know it."

Needless to say, chills covered my body when I heard those words. I am sure the look on my face was that of disbelief and astonishment. For a moment, I was frozen in the very spot where I was standing. I couldn't have been moved with a bulldozer at that point.

"Many of them children belonged to the railroad workers or servants," he added.

Still, I could not force any part of my body to move. "Boo!" screamed my friend as she jumped out from behind one of foundation pillars. "Aha! I scared you! I scared you," she sang as I was finally able to breathe and take control of my stature once more.

George was already at the front porch by now and slowly climbing the front steps. I was still silently calling him "George," and it seemed to suit him. Poor guy, he had no idea. But being raised in the South, he must have known that he was being rude by not introducing himself or telling us his name. Anyway, our tour continued from there.

We continued our adventure and took the entire tour of the home—a very slow tour of the entire house, I might add! He just didn't get in any type of hurry.

As we entered the gentlemen's room, George slowly opened the large pocket doors. They disappeared as they slid into the walls to become hidden; this amazed me. It was an architectural masterpiece! I caught a whiff of the distinct smell of sweet yet bitter pipe smoke, or maybe it was a cigar. In either case, it was a familiar aroma, as my grandfather would sometimes smoke cherry-flavored tobacco in his pipe. I'm not a fan at all of cigarette or cigar smoke, but my granddaddy's pipe—ah, I loved that smell! This comforted me, and I then almost felt cozy. I was relaxing now and enjoying the tour.

We were then led upstairs where there were four large bedrooms. I heard a deep and winded cough. I suggested that we not disturb anyone upstairs and that we could get the rest of the tour at a later date, if necessary. Both my friend and George turned to look at me as if I were crazy. "What are you talking about?" asked my friend.

"There's no one else in the house but us," said George (still unaware of his new name I had silently given him).

I heard the cough again. "See?" I said loudly and insistently. "There *is* somebody up here!" I hurried to the front room where the door was open. "It's coming from in here!" As I looked into the room, I saw the bed was neatly made and the room was tidy. It had a bed and a chest of drawers alongside a desk and chair. But there was no one in the room—at least no one that the human eye could apparently see!

"That there's the room where William McGowan died," said George as he pointed to the room with his walking cane. "He was General McGowan's son," he added. "Died of pneumonia," said George. "He was only thirty-nine years old."

My friend and I both stood motionless. "Stop kidding around," she said to me with a nervous laugh as if trying to dismiss the situation.

I was in no way joking. I *know* what I heard, and I was as serious as I could be! That strange feeling came over me again, as did the goose bumps; they were back and all over my body.

At this point, as far as I was concerned, this tour was *over*, and I quickly headed downstairs. My friend was close behind me. As I reached the bottom of the stairs, back on the bottom landing, the gentleman yelled, "Hey!" as he leaned over the top floor wooden railing of the staircase and chuckled his distinct laugh again.

I stopped. "Yes, sir?" I asked as I looked up.

"I just wanted you to know, my name ain't George." He let out another loud cackle, and I was out of there faster than an eight-legged horse at the starting line of a race.

We. Were. Gone!

As my friend and I got back into the car to leave, I was still a little shaken. We drove out of the driveway around the neighboring church and parked in a parking space on the town square. We then began to review our photos on our digital camera. *None* of my photos took! *All* my photos were black! My friend's photos turned out very blurry, for the most part, but she did get a few good shots. Some of her photos had light anomalies and orbs; others had distinct blurs and shadows we could not explain.

We never went back, and we never saw George again— nor did we want to!

~

The apparition of William McGowan has reportedly been seen on countless occasions, usually in the front, upstairs, rounded window that faces Main Street in Abbeville. He has also been caught on digital cameras standing in the window. Phantom coughs have also been heard and recorded by local paranormal investigation teams. Visitors to the historic home/museum have also heard the phantom cough and smelled the aroma of tobacco being smoked.

THE HIDDEN CELLAR

A local paranormal team was invited to investigate the McGowan House, also known as the General's House. They were filming a sizzle reel for a pitch to a national television station about haunted Southern towns, and they had heard that this dwelling was reputedly haunted, so they'd come to check it out.

A member of the historical society would act as their tour guide and chaperone as they filmed in the historic home.

The group asked to go into the creepiest part of the home to conduct their investigation. They were led to the middle area in the back of the house. "This is something that not many people even know exists," explained the tour guide. He moved a rug to reveal a wooden floor. In a certain manner, he opened the wooden floor and revealed what appeared to be a dark abyss. The smell of mildew or must filled the air when the pit was opened. "Is this the basement?" one of the camera crew members asked.

"Nope, this is not the basement. It's the secret root cellar," the guide explained. There were several hidden steps that gave access to the musty square hole.

The plan was to allow the "sensitive" one of the group, the medium, to enter first. Without any knowledge of the room, she would write down what she sensed, and after the evidence of the investigation, she would compare her notes to the findings. What follows is the medium's personal experience, in her own words.

Of course, I am not usually frightened very easily. It takes a lot to spook me. Me being me, I was excited to head straight down into the cellar, but I had to be careful. It was obvious that no one had been down there in a long time. I knew the others would eventually follow after I conducted my walk-through, so I headed on in. I began to slowly and carefully descend the staircase, which was less than ten steps. With each step down that I took, the colder, damper, and mustier the air got. With this being a root cellar, that would appear to be normal, I thought. After about the third step, I felt the wisp of a large spiderweb encase my face. I am *not* a fan of spiders, mind you, but I was on a mission. I then used the flash of my camera to see where I was going. It was a small, cold, musty, square room with a seemingly misplaced wall covering what looked like some sort of tunnel that was being dug out at one point—and it seemed to lead to, well, nowhere!

A shiver passed over my body as I felt something brush up against the hem of my long shirt. I really couldn't see much of anything, so I turned on the flashlight of my cell phone to look around, as my camera batteries were quickly drained and went dead. I had a feeling I was not alone, and even with a flashlight, I would not be able to see who or what was in there with me. At this point, I *knew* whatever or whoever it was, was not of the physical world. As I looked down to see what was now holding on to my shirt, I could see nothing but my shirt being tugged. As a "sensitive," I closed my eyes so I could "see." I then saw a transparent little girl with blond hair, ringlets of curls held in place by a rather thick blue ribbon tied in a perfect bow. She looked as if she were in her sleepwear. It was a long white nightgown, and her feet were bare. She couldn't have been more than three or four years old. "John," she said as she reached up toward me, as if asking me to pick her up. Suddenly, right beside me appeared a large, middle-aged African-American male. He was wearing brown suspenders over the shoulders of a long-sleeved white cotton shirt, dark work pants, boots (with his pant legs tucked in), and an old straw hat.

"Hey, John," said the little girl as she looked up to him with a smile and placed her tiny hand in his large hand.

"Where are we going?" The large man never answered the tiny girl. He turned to pick her up, as if he had taken care of her a million times, and it was obvious they were on a mission and in hiding for their safety. Once the little girl was in his arms, he walked right through me as if I did not exist. He and the little girl slowly disappeared into that mysterious tunnel that had been partially dug out behind the wall of the root cellar.

At this point, my energy, as well as my flashlight batteries, was completely drained. As the apparition walked through me, it was like I was in a different place and time. I could feel all their emotions at one time: happy, sad, fearful, yet safe. This was one of the most extreme experiences I have ever had, physically, emotionally, and spiritually. Bizarre is the only word that comes close to describing what happened that night. But when it was all over with, I was strangely at peace. I felt what I sensed them feeling: safe. This root cellar felt as if it were utilized as a safe hiding place that gained many people to safety. My sense was that John was the little girl's protector and that he was taking her to her loved one in a place where no harm could come to her. They apparently had to escape the area during the night based on what the little girl was wearing.

I returned to the stairs to let the others know I had completed the walk-through and made my way back up to the main floor of the house and began to write down my experience in my notes.

The investigation continued as three other members of the paranormal team filled the small area. The next step of the investigation commenced with an EVP (electronic voice phenomena) session. This is where questions are intentionally asked out loud on a recording device to see if any responses can be captured on a recording. A voice recorder is used to record noises, voices, and sounds that the human ear cannot normally hear. After an investigation is completed, the recordings are reviewed and listened to carefully with earphones or headsets to see if any response was given to questions, conversations, or in silence during an investigation. At a later date, that is called the reveal; the evidence, if any, is revealed to the owner of the property or the person who initially requested the investigation.

At the conclusion of the investigation that night, the secret doorway was closed, and the team had not returned.

In reviewing the voice recordings, an EVP was captured. Sounds of a little child giggling were heard, as was the voice of a young child calling the name of "John."

This evidence was revealed to the tour guide several weeks later. The tour guide said there were no stories of a little girl or the man that was described, but he shared that during the war there were so many people hiding out, and there were hundreds of deaths by illnesses in those days, that he would not question anything that may lurk in and around Abbeville.

This home has since been investigated by several other paranormal teams, each of which has collected very interesting EVPs of coughing, giggling, and footsteps via digital voice recorders.

Over the years, the Abbeville Ghost Tour is held annually by the local chamber of commerce, and most every year, this home is a featured stop on the tour.

CHAPTER 4
Ghosts of Belmont Inn

During the 1800s and 1900s, Abbeville was a busy railroad hub. Workers on the trains and the railroads needed a place to stay for the night when overnight stops were made in Abbeville. Traveling salesmen that were known as "tinkers" also needed a place to stay when they came into town, so it was more than obvious that Abbeville needed a hotel, and it needed to be a large one!

In 1901, the idea of a hotel was the conception of a local Abbeville business man Mr. P. Rosenberg. In 1902, construction began, and in 1903, the Eureka Hotel was completed. Nicknamed appropriately as the "$30,000 hotel" (as that is how much it would ultimately cost to erect), a formal grand opening took place on August 19, 1903.

Originally offering thirty-four guest rooms, the Eureka also had numerous public restrooms that were outfitted with baths; a few lovely sitting meeting parlors; unique shops; a dining room that was most elegant; and a sample room on the ground floor that served as a display area for the traveling salesman to show their goods to local merchants, passersby, and travelers.

The three-story hotel would now accommodate such patrons as railroad workers, traveling acting troops (during and after the Vaudeville era), musicians, and visitors of a higher social status (those who could afford to stay in a hotel). Business was booming for the overnight venue, and life was indeed grand in Abbeville, South Carolina.

It wasn't until between the 1920s and 1950s that the hotel started to transition. The name was changed to the Belmont Hotel. During the 1950s, a young man by the name of Frank Fleming was hired as a bellboy. Eventually, this bellboy would become the owner of the hotel, and it would be transformed into a semi-residential inn for the elderly during the late fifties.

The 1970s brought heartache to many as the hotel closed its doors and fell into almost total disrepair. It seemed that the days of splendor were over forever. Walls were deteriorating, and floors were falling in. The damage over the next decade was then believed to be in total disrepair. Many thought the building would be leveled or imploded, as it was a safety hazard and nearly dilapidated. However, in the early 1980s, talk of restoration emerged and was put into action. On November 23, 1984, what is now known as the Belmont Inn had a grand reopening, offering twenty-five rooms, each with their own private bath, modern accommodations, and conveniences. It was a rebirth for the old building! During this renovation, unique features that are still intact today are that of the entrances and doorways that were created by the skills of a seasoned master cabinetmaker. All are unique and one of a kind.

The mid-1990s was yet another downfall for the now infamous hotel. In 1995, it was closed yet again, but in 1996, the hotel was purchased by Alan and Audrey Peterson. They kept the original outward appearance, including the marble veranda area and the slate roof. Antique furnishings on the inside of the estate still presented a sense of nostalgia. Marble terrazzo floors added to the authentic antiquated hotel, as did handcrafted armoires in each guest room.

The inn has changed hands many times over the decades, and on October 6, 2008, it went up for auction under the ownership of Fred Rhans but was returned to him in his name on that same day.

In 2013, a German couple became the new owners and innkeepers, but the hotel went into foreclosure in 2015 when the couple went separate ways. Still known as the Belmont Inn, the hotel would change hands yet again.

Edie New and Ren'ee Smith most recently invested in the property and are now not only the current owners, they serve as the hostesses and innkeepers. These two ladies have literally brought the inn back to the prestigious and cozy life it so deserves.

Today, the main level, which is actually the second floor, is made up of a common room, a wine room, a dining area, and guest rooms. The third floor is made up of rooms alone. There have been many updates to the hotel rooms, including high-speed Internet, hair dryers, new bedding and mattresses, and refinished floors to highlight the heart of the pine hardwoods.

The basement of the inn has served several different purposes over the last few decades, and a portion of the basement has always housed and still currently houses the pub of the hotel. Known as "Tinker's Alley," it was named for the many traveling salesmen who would display their goods that were sold to local merchants and passersby. Tinker's Alley is located in the front side of the basement, and the entrance door faces East Pickens Street. Located on the slant of a hill, the facing road runs between The Abbeville Opera House and the historic inn. The basement is now also the location of the registration desk, the gift shop, a small laundry area, a conference/meeting room, restrooms, a storage area, and even a dog-grooming business.

One thing you may want to remember is that when you check in or book your reservation, please do not ask to stay in room number thirteen, as there isn't one!

"Guests will notice the absence of room thirteen in keeping with tall tales of superstition," said owner Edie New, as she and co-owner Ren'ee Smith elected to continue that tradition. Upon counting guest rooms, there are only twenty-five—not twenty-six.

A very prominent horse statue that stands in the front of the Belmont Inn was donated by the estate of Dr. Walter Bishop, a well-respected physician who called Abbeville his home during his last days.

For over a century now, this hotel has been a landmark not only in Abbeville, but for the entire state of South Carolina.

"Some rooms even come with a ghost," shared New when asked what makes the Belmont so unique. She made this statement with a slight tilt of her head, serious tone in her voice, eyebrows raised, and in a very matter-of-fact way. No laughter accompanied her answer. Edie also elaborated by sharing that she has personally experienced ghostly and/or unexplained happenings in the hotel since she and Re'nee took ownership. "Especially when changes are being made and renovations are taking place," she added.

So whether you are the type of person who seeks out haunted hotels (in hopes that you can spot an apparition with your own eyes or maybe a disembodied voice on your own handheld voice recorder) or you are like many other guests who want to stay in a very historic hotel, one thing is for sure, this beautifully decorated haven will not disappoint!

Here are a few of the stories as shared by several people who have claimed to have experiences in the Belmont Inn.

THE WANDERING WIDOW

The back entrance to the Belmont Inn was once the laundry area but is now the location of the registration desk. On several occasions, a lady in a long, black, full-lace dress has been seen wandering in this area.

No one really knows who she is or why she just wanders, but she has reportedly been seen many times over the last few decades.

She is described as having a lace veil over her face, and she even wears black lace gloves. Some say she looks as if she is either coming from or heading to a funeral. Her dress is that of the Victorian era and includes a bustle.

One evening, as a guest of the Belmont stepped off the elevator and turned right to exit into the parking area, she saw the wandering lady pass right beside her and then disappear into the wall between the restrooms on the bottom floor.

"She just passed right by me and went right into the wall!" explained the startled guest, who asked to remain anonymous. "It was almost like she was floating. I never saw her feet, only her long, flowing lace dress. I couldn't see her face because she had a very long veil covering it. It [the veil] was as long in the front as it was in the back." The guest explained that she never felt afraid, just taken aback, as she had never before even believed in ghosts. "But I do now!" she concluded with a rather nervous but convincing laugh. The eyewitness said she would have no problem staying at the historic inn in the future. "It is still one of my favorite hotels," she concluded, but insisted that she would utilize the front door on the second floor during her future visits.

This "Wandering Widow" seems to have the aspects of what is referred to as a residual haunting. This type of haunting is very much like an old moving filmstrip that plays over and over. It is not known exactly when or why the spiritual filmstrip is played. Some residual hauntings are believed to occur on the anniversary of a tragedy, while others "replay" over and over at the same time each day. A full moon is also believed by some to trigger such ghostly sightings.

For now, the story of the wandering widow remains one of the most mysterious ghost sightings in Abbeville.

ABRAHAM

Abraham was known to be the friendliest and most de-voted doorman to have ever worked at the Belmont Inn.

Of average build, he was an older black gentleman who, though no longer walking on the earth, still resides at the hotel in spirit. Known for his big smile and passion for serving others, Abraham has been seen in all areas of the hotel, but most often in the common room on the top floor, by the front door that opens onto the big front porch of the hotel.

Abraham had been taught not to speak unless spoken to, but with his wide, friendly face, many spoke and told Abraham hello. He was adamant about always opening the door for any and all guests, whether male or female. He seemed to want to serve everyone to the best of his ability.

Doors in the historic hotel have been known to open and close apparently on their own. Doorknobs have also reportedly been shaken, as Abraham would check each door every night to ensure the safety of each guest.

If ever you are a guest at the Belmont Inn and you hear a doorknob rattle or a door open and shut with no one visibly there, be assured that it may be the doorman Abraham watching out for you and your family's safety.

MISS MAY BELL

"If you wants to make people happy, you needs to feed 'em" is what the ghost of Miss May Bell has been known for saying at the inn. May Bell is the spirit of an older African-American cook who has been in the kitchen area of the hotel. She has been known to move and hide knives as well. Knives have reportedly been found in the freezer and in the oven for no apparent reason. Miss May Bell also likes to supervise in the kitchen, and her apparition has reportedly been seen only on a few occasions, but always in the kitchen or around a table full of guests. She apparently also loved people and enjoyed serving others.

THE LOST NECKLACE

The following story is told by a resident of Greenwood, South Carolina.

~

On a late evening in December, I attended a year-end awards ceremony for my place of employment that was held in the dining room on the second floor of the Belmont Inn.

My husband and I entered the hotel through the side door on the basement level and took the elevator to the main floor. The bartender directed us to the elevator and stairs and said the choice was ours as to which one we would like to utilize. He then stated that there would be directional signs to point the way once we reached the second/main floor. We chose to utilize the elevator. Once we reached the next level and stepped off of the elevator, I noticed a tall, well-dressed lady wearing a long, baby-blue Victorian dress. One could tell that it was tailor-made, as it fit her hourglass figure perfectly. She was also wearing a rather large, matching, wide-brimmed hat that tied around her chin. Lace gloves covered her hands, and she was holding a closed white parasol. She simply stood at the foot of the staircase as if looking frantically for something. As we passed by, she turned and seemed to look straight through my husband and me as if we were not even there. The look on her face was that of panic and sadness. She then turned her head to the right as if to look up to toward the top of the grand staircase, one step at a time. It was apparent that she had lost something very valuable. I uttered a friendly Southern, "Hey, how are you?" and we continued walking toward our destination. My husband gave me the strangest look, and he asked me who I was talking to. "That reenactor at the stairs," I answered, and he gave me yet another strange look, but he didn't ask any more questions as we followed the directional signs and finally reached our destination.

The incident puzzled me during our dinner engagement, and my husband insisted I was seeing things, because he hadn't witnessed any such lady.

I couldn't help but wonder if she ever found what she was looking for, but I hope she did. Over and over in my mind, I wondered about what I had seen. I just summed it up as a reenactor or actress who was about to head to the neighboring opera house for her performance in a play. *That must be what it was,* I continued to try to convince myself.

After dinner, I excused myself for a restroom break before we headed home. At that time, I met one of the concierges of the establishment. When I asked him about it, he explained to me that there is a ghost story in the hotel about a lady who lost her most valuable necklace and still, even in the afterlife, searches for it. "She has been seen here a lot." He giggled. "I haven't seen her, but a lot of people say they have! She's usually right around the grand staircase," he concluded.

CHARLIE'S ROOM

A Civil War soldier is believed to haunt what is now room number ten at the inn. The story, as shared with the author, was that a soldier who had served in the Civil War had just come home to Abbeville. He had been away for several years. His name is not known, but he has most commonly been called "Charlie."

Charlie was out for a stroll on the square on a hot summer's day. An altercation ensued between the local sheriff and a citizen. Charlie had witnessed the altercation and believed the sheriff was wrong (the sheriff supposedly beat the citizen nearly to death during the altercation). Charlie was said to have shot the sheriff as a way of defending the (what he believed to be innocent) citizen. In turn, another man who was a bystander shot Charlie, believing to be defending the sheriff. Bleeding profusely, Charlie made his way up the hotel steps and into a room where he soon died.

It is not sure what the exact layout of the original hotel was when this incident occurred, but what is now known as room number ten is where the paranormal activity seems to be most noticeable. Items have reportedly moved on their own accord, groans of a man who seems to be in pain have been heard, and indentions on the bed have been seen (as if someone were sitting on the bed) with no one physically or visibly there.

OTHER HAUNTED ROOMS

Reputedly, over the years, there have been several rooms that have had paranormal activity reported at the Belmont Inn. As stated before, not knowing the original layout of the hotel, it is most certain that the room numbers of today were not the same as when the inn was originally constructed. Therefore, the haunted room numbers that are mentioned in this book may very well not be the same room number that is referred to in the following pages.

On January 23, 2003, a psychic from Alabama visited the inn and at one in the morning performed an automatic writing in room number twenty-four. Automatic writing is defined as an individual who communicates with spirits allowing those spirits to utilize a writing instrument (such as a pen or pencil) that is held by the medium himself. This psychic medium spoke of a miller by the name of Samuel Johnson who had a quick temper.

The next evening, Friday, January 24, 2003, in room number fourteen, again at one in the morning, the automatic writing told of a woman by the name of Matilda who had come into the city. She was warned by her father of men in the city. She felt as if no one loved her. During two other automatic writings, at nine in the morning the same day, a spirit by the name of John insists that there are about fifty entities that reside and/or visit the inn. Later, John said there were specifically forty-three spirits who inhabit the inn.

Most recently, the following room numbers (as numbered most recently) have reportedly had odd occurrences that have yet to be explained: ten, seventeen, eighteen, twenty-two, twenty-three, twenty-four, and twenty-six.

THE BUSINESS MAN

Here is the story of yet another ghostly sighting at the inn, as told by a former employee of the inn.

~

I was working the front desk and rounded the staircase to enter the banquet room. I remember that when I entered the grand room, I noticed a distinguished-looking gentleman wearing a derby hat and a fitted, gray, three-piece suit. He was leaning against the mantle with a cigar in his mouth. He was sporting a dark beard and a handlebar mustache. I could distinctly smell that awful cigar he was smoking; however, I did not *see* any smoke. I thought that to be odd. He was looking at a pocket watch that was attached to his suit pocket by a chain. He looked like one of those rich men that you see in an old Western movie. As he raised his head, he had a stern, almost angry, look on his face, and our eyes met. I quickly looked away, as I was sure that he could not be angry with me! Being raised in the South, my mama had always taught me that staring was rude and that is just something I should never do. By then, my shift replacement was coming in the front door. I glanced back to see that the angry man was once again looking down at his pocket watch, seemingly more agitated than before. I turned to catch up with my coworker, whom I pulled to the side so it would be obvious to the man that I was talking about him. "Do you know that man standing over by the mantle? Or why he is here? And why would he be dressed like that?" I asked my coworker.

"Who?" my coworker asked. "Who are you talking about? What man? There's nobody in that room!" my co-worker insisted as he walked away and shook his head.

"He's right there," I said as I pointed him out—but the man was gone. He had simply disappeared. I have never stepped foot back in there.

THE BELLHOP OF THE BELMONT

Many people believe that when an old building is renovated, spirits that inhabit that building may get "stirred up" and become active and/or more active than usual. Though this may or may not be true at this historic hotel, the present owners Ren'ee Smith and Edie New are convinced that ghostly activity happens whether or not there are any changes going on.

Although there are several entities that are believed to reside in the inn, none of them have ever seemed to harm anyone. The story of the bellhop of the Belmont seems to be a residual haunting. There are many variations of his story, this one being by a patron who met in Tinker's Alley for a late dinner with her friends.

~

It was a cold winter's evening, and my friends and I were meeting in the basement/bar area of the Belmont Inn for a late dinner. It was so cold that we could see our breath each time we exhaled in the cold winter air. As I walked inside of the side entrance door from the sidewalk, the atmosphere of the bar (which is more like a restaurant with a bar area, in my opinion) was very welcoming and cozy, and it was warm. The bare brick wall on the right side of the room gave a sense of nostalgia. It felt good. Several small square tables with accompanying chairs seemed to await our arrival. Jazz music was playing lightly, which enhanced the ambiance even more. The lighting was low, but each table had a candle that gave off a perfect glow and just enough light to see everyone around me.

As we all joined in to move a few tables together, we made what appeared to be a long, majestic table suited for royalty, and now there was room for all eleven of us to be seated. Glancing at the menu that our waiter had brought over to us, we were all starving and ready for a good meal. After deciding on what to order, I placed the menu on the table in front of me and noticed that even though I had been in the restaurant for over ten minutes and warmed up, I felt a shiver go through my body. I thought that was odd but simply put my jacket back on.

While my fellow dinner guests continued to make their selections, I saw a dark shadow move from the bar area to the brick wall. It happened very quickly and looked to be about the size of an average-sized adult. I dismissed it as someone at our table who had moved his arm near the candle, which must have created a shadow upon the wall.

I thought no more of it and excused myself to go to the restroom. On the way to the restroom, I began to admire and read the old movie posters that were hung about. Artwork from local artists as well as a simple mirror adorned the walls and was very tastefully done, I might add. The pub was in the back of the restaurant, and though very small, the U-shaped bar had about a dozen stools that held a few patrons.

I turned the corner and entered the restroom door. As I finished washing my hands and reached for a paper towel, I looked up to glance in the mirror. As I did, I caught a glance of a lady dressed in all black behind me. I knew I had not heard the door open or close, so I was confused as to whom it could be. When I turned my head, I saw no one. "Hello?" I said as another shiver fell over my body. "Hellooooo?" I asked again. No response. Nothing. I turned back to the mirror, but all I saw was my very own reflection this time. By this time, I was freezing, even with my jacket on. As I exhaled, my cold breath fogged up a spot on the mirror. Needless to say, I was terrified and threw the used paper towel at the wastebasket, which I am certain I did not hit, but I wasn't about to go back and pick it up. I was more than spooked and could not get the door open fast enough! Shivering, I made my way back to my chair at the dinner table as fast as my legs would take me. I was out of breath but felt much better when I was among my peers. I was relieved when the waiter placed my salad in front of me. For a moment, I thought I was losing my mind. But I *know* what I saw! I just couldn't logically explain it.

My night out with my friends continued as all of our entrees arrived. We laughed, we sang, we danced, and we ate a delicious meal.

As the night began to wind down, a few people left from our table and a few more regulars trickled in to sit at the bar. Again, I began to shiver. As I turned my head back to my right, toward the door from where we entered, I noticed there was a somewhat transparent man who was wearing an old-fashioned bellhop uniform. He was just standing there beside the brick wall (which I could actually see in detail through his body). I sat motionless and wanted to so desperately ask my friends if they too could see him, but it was as if I were frozen. I could not speak. I could not move. I suddenly had tunnel vision and could only see him, yet it was obvious he could not see me.

He was a young, handsome, African-American man in his early to mid-twenties, and along with his grayish-blue bellhop uniform, he was wearing white gloves. I distinctly remember his white gloves. It was as if he were in his own little world and did not know that anyone else was in the room. He stood there, motionless, with his hands by his side. It was as if he were waiting on someone. His face had a happy yet anxious smile upon it. His demeanor assured me that he was a nice, friendly, hard-working man who was happy and excited. Still, he just stood there, looking out toward the road that runs between the pub and its neighboring opera house. He was staring straight through what is now the entrance door, waiting, watching in nervous anticipation. My friend Michael called my name, which startled me and broke the trance I had apparently fallen into. "More tea?" asked my waiter.

"Oh yes, sorry, yeah," I said as I composed myself and came back to reality. After he poured me some more tea, I quickly looked back over to the spot where I had seen the ghostly figure. He had disappeared. He was gone—just *gone!*

"Did you see that?" I whispered to my friend seated directly beside me.

"See what?" she answered before taking a sip of her water.

"There was a man over there. He was wearing an old bellhop uniform. Did you see him?" I asked a little more urgently yet in the same whisper.

"No, I didn't see anything," my friend answered as she took out her camera to take a picture. "Didn't see a thing!

Hey, everybody, look this way and smile," she added, fixated on capturing the group photo of the night. She was the shutterbug of the group, to say the least.

The evening further progressed with laughter, a few more songs around the piano, and warm bellies from a delicious dinner. It was almost time for the bar to close, and we were all saying our goodbyes. I kept looking over to the brick wall, but I never saw the young man again.

Before I left, I was determined to get an explanation of what I had witnessed. I had to convince myself that I was not going crazy! I made it a point to go back to the restroom, but this time, I asked a friend to go with me, telling her of the incident in the restroom. She gave me a strange look and checked the stalls before I would use the restroom for a second time. She laughed at me and asked what kind of "tea" I had been drinking.

I knew no one would believe me, so I didn't share the happenings with anyone else. I decided I would ask the waiter about the strange goings-on. So, as the others were gathering their coats and saying their goodbyes, I asked the waiter about the transparent man I thought—no, *knew*—I had seen.

As I described him, the waiter gave me a rather crooked little smile, a strange look with one of his eyebrows raised, but then said with a chuckle, "Oh, that's the bellhop. I've never seen him, but some people say it is the ghost a young bellhop who used to work here in the early days." The waiter proceeded to tell me the story of a young white woman who would visit her family in Abbeville, and though she was never a guest at the hotel, she would come into town with her aunt to shop and have lunch at the hotel.

When the bellhop was off work from the hotel, he would work at the local stores around the square, loading up merchandise for customers. On one occasion, it is believed that he had helped carry merchandise for the young woman's aunt and he had caught the young woman's eye; not too long after, he captured her heart.

Knowing that that their interracial love was forbidden (as they were in the old South and of different races) did not change how they felt. They had unexpectedly and unintentionally fallen in love.

They would hide away and meet in the basement to spend time together. Not willing to sacrifice their hearts, the two young lovers decided to run away so they could be together. The plan was for the young woman to meet him at midnight with her family's horse and buggy. He would wear his bellhop uniform and act as driver for her. They were to travel up north, where they could be together.

As the young woman was leaving the house, her cousin, to whom she had told of the affair, was awakened by the sound of the buggy leaving, as the stable was located on the side of the house and below her bedroom window. The cousin watched as the infatuated woman drove quietly and ever so slowly toward town so as not to be caught. The cousin knew this was yet another rendezvous that she had so desperately tried to stop. The cousin ran to wake her father, who quickly jumped on his horse and followed his niece into town. The uncle intercepted the meeting, and instead of meeting and running away with the bellhop, the young woman was labeled as a harlot who had shamed her family. She was immediately sent back to her hometown before sunrise. Never again was she allowed to visit her family in Abbeville. Never again did her family members in Abbeville speak to her. Never did the young woman marry.

It was rumored that the young woman's family had the young man killed in the very spot where he was watching and waiting for his forbidden love. He was never seen in Abbeville again, nor was his body ever found. He seemed to just disappear off the face of the earth.

"Right here in Tinker's Alley," explained the waiter, "is where they were going to meet and run away, so apparently, over a century later…he still waits."

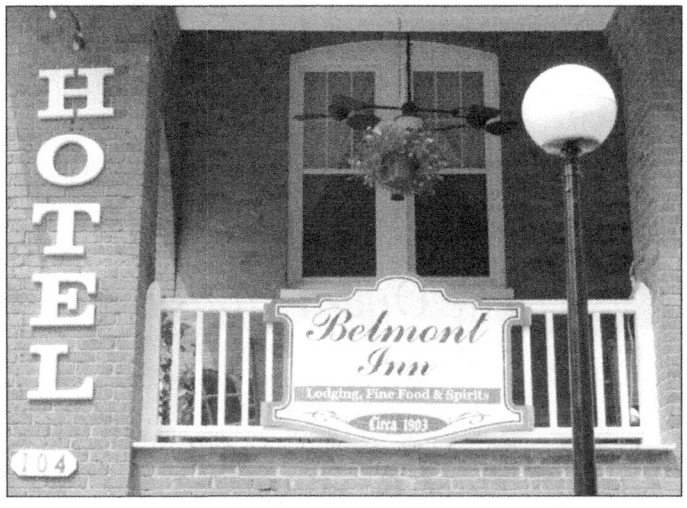

CHAPTER 5

The Opera House

In the early 1900s, turn-of-the-century traveling road companies (acting/entertainment) would produce shows in New York City, and once a show was complete and ready to perform, groups of entertainers and actors would go on the road, traveling up and down the East Coast to entertain thousands of patrons in their local theatres and opera houses.

Abbeville was considered the halfway point between Richmond, Virginia, and Atlanta, Georgia, and the road companies would stop in Abbeville to rest for the night. Citizens of Abbeville decided it would be a good idea to construct a theatre there so when the entertainers stayed in Abbeville, they could also possibly perform in Abbeville. They took the proper steps of establishing such a venue in 1900 by submitting their request in writing to a Vaudeville Circuit that was based in New York City. By 1908, their wish was granted as the grand opening of The Abbeville Opera House took place, with *The Great Divide* being the very first production.

Statistics that are kept by the theatre show that between the years 1908 and 1913, patrons enjoyed over 260 live productions. From 1914 to 1930, there were still live performances, but over 3,200 moving pictures were shown.

Over the years, the opera house boasts of performances by such greats as Jimmy Durante and Fanny Brice. George White's Ziegfeld Follies and Scandals were also among the famous performances. Most recently, late television star and magician Harry Anderson.

By 1927, movies became the main attractions, and gradually, the live entertainment and road shows ceased. Until the late 1950s, the "Opera House," as now known to residents, became a movie theater only and, sadly, was eventually closed.

In May of 1968, the efforts of George W. Settles, concerned citizens, and the American Community Theatre came to fruition as the theatre was restored and again up and running with live performances. By 1970, performance competitions were held on the stage.

Tourism increased in Abbeville in late 1970s, and Michael Genevie, along with his professional touring theatre company, decided to make the Abbeville Opera House their home.

For over three decades, Genevie has not only kept the doors open, but served as executive director to the opera house. Genevie also shared his talents of acting, singing, and directing with the audiences of the historic theatre. Under his direction, the Abbeville Opera House is proud to have been designated the official state theatre of South Carolina. Numerous awards have been earned by the theatre, and among those is the prestigious South Carolina Governor's Travel Award for Tourism, which they have been awarded twice. The Abbeville City Hall offices are also currently located in the theatre.

The Abbeville Opera House is listed on the National Register of Historic Places, and other than the addition of rocking seats and air conditioning, the Opera House has been fully restored to its original condition.

The 7,500-square-foot stage is now known as the "Michael Genevie Mainstage," and the seating area is known as the "George W. Settles Auditorium." Both areas of the theatre were appropriately named after the two gentlemen who put the word "live" back into the performances at the historic Abbeville Opera House. Thanks to these two men and numerous members of a community who cared, thousands of patrons (local, as well as those from afar) continue to enjoy live theatre in Abbeville, South Carolina.

ENCORE!

There are three ghost stories that are affiliated with the historic theatre known as the Abbeville Opera House. The most famous ghost story is one of a young woman who haunts the Abbeville Opera House.

In 1914, a road company had traveled from up north to perform at the Abbeville Opera House in Upstate South Carolina; the group of ninety included actors, actresses, and chorus members who were to perform the ever so popular production of *Ben-Hur*. In addition to the troop were several live horses that pulled the chariots across the grand stage.

With each stop in Abbeville, the members of the group would stay at what was then known as the Eureka Hotel, presently known as the Belmont Inn.

The troupes would come in on a Wednesday, set up the stage props, and perform a run-through/rehearsal.

Live performances for patrons would be on Thursday, Friday, and Saturday.

With everything on schedule for this particular performance, a beautiful, young female chorus member fell ill after the Wednesday night rehearsal. She was sent back to the hotel to rest for the upcoming performances in the days to follow. Feeling better, the young woman made her way over to the opera house and took a seat in the balcony section. She was able to catch the last scene of the performance. It was said that she led the standing ovation for the performance that night and then returned to her room, where her condition worsened and she ultimately died in her sleep.

Her spirit is said to haunt the theatre through the faint yet bright lights during curtain calls immediately after a performance. She is seen standing, applauding, and smiling. She is always described to be a very attractive young woman in a long colonial dress. Others have said that she has been seen peering through an open window that looks down over the stage from a dressing room above, yet again, always smiling.

A chair has been placed on the third-floor balcony that is described as being different from all of the other balcony chairs. A light is also left on for her in that area.

According to theatre employees, if her chair is moved even a fraction of an inch or if the light is not left on for her, she becomes unhappy and tends to make unusual things happen. Hearing her voice is not uncommon, and she has even been seen in the restroom closest to her chair.

Patrons, volunteers, employees, and even the actors have reportedly seen this young woman's apparition on numerous occasions.

BEHIND THE SCENES

In 1908, the completion of the Abbeville Opera House took place, and the doors were finally open. However, during the construction of the theatre, a male construction worker was on top of the seventy-foot back wall when he accidentally fell to his death. His name is not known, but he is said to make the historic theatre his spiritual home, and he, as one can very well see, is a bit of a prankster!

Odd things have been known to happen before, during, and after live performances at the Abbeville Opera House. As far back as anyone can remember, props have been known to be moved and/or simply disappear, only to reappear moments later or reappear in another part of the theatre where they never should have been. Feelings of being watched while no else is around are also a common occurrence. Heavy ropes in the pulled rigging system have been known to sway when no one can be seen near them. Shadows that seem to be seen in the peripheral area of actors backstage and in the dressing room are yet further paranormal activity. "Cold spots," many times, accompany those said shadows. Banging on pipes seems to be yet another jovial pastime that is believed to be performed by this mischievous poltergeist. Many believe the spirit of a construction worker is to blame for all, or at least most, of these occurrences.

JOE

The third ghostly apparition that is said to haunt the historic opera house is that of a big and broad-shouldered African-American man dressed in work clothes. His heavy footsteps have been heard throughout the theatre. It is believed that this is the ghost of a man who was actually murdered in the theatre, but no name has been linked to such a murder in the building or to this gentleman, as described. He just wanders around, oblivious to any living person around him. He is believed to be a residual haunting, as he has been seen in the upstairs restroom area, always walking from one side of the room to the other, disappearing right into the wall. He has also been seen from the streets down below, in front of the opera house, peering down from the far right-facing window. The origin of this apparition is not known; however, more than one paranormal group has, from their evidence, become convinced that his name is "Joe."

CHAPTER 6

The Painted Lady

There are very few steamboat houses left in the United States, yet Abbeville is proud to say that one of them calls it home. Designed to resemble a steamboat, the "Painted Lady" (as named by her current owner) is adorned with a staircase on both sides (on the outside) of the house. Located on Main Street, this house was at one time also referred to and known as the Visanska Castle. She was built in 1882 upon a foundation that had once before held another grand home, but unfortunately was lost to a fire.

This home is said to house much more than just antique furniture and memories; she is also made up of secret hiding places, important historical happenings, and even documented paranormal activity, including sightings of full apparitions. It also has historical significance. When Confederate President Jefferson Davis signed the dissolution of the Civil War, it was upon this property where his accompanying troops and some of his cabinet members stayed for the night.

Over the decades, the Painted Lady has been more than just a private home. It has also been known to be a boarding house for railroad workers and solders. This home is listed on the National Historic Register and in present day is a private home to a single owner. Renovations are currently underway, and the bottom floor is used as a residence while the top floor is under reconstruction.

The Painted Lady is a most interesting piece of property and has her share of ghostly happenings. Over the next few pages are a few of those encounters that the owner of the home has given us permission to share.

A GHOSTLY WALTZ

On a hot summer's day just a few years back, a young couple had made plans to visit their friend in Abbeville. Hugs and handshakes were the common greetings in the South, and that is just how the reunion had begun. Sweet tea, ice water, or a cold beer was the choice as the three friends sat on the old wicker furniture that adorned the wide front porch. Reminiscing, dinner, and lots of laughter filled the evening that eventually turned into night, and even though the full moon filled the porch with enough light to remain until dawn, the trio decided to call it a night.

The guests had showered and finally settled down for the night in the guest room. Just a few minutes later, they both began to hear old music, music that was accompanied by a bit of scratchy static; it sounded like old waltz music. They decided to just lie there and go to sleep.

The music didn't stop. It continued on and on, to the point where they decided to get up out of bed and find out where it was coming from. Walking into the next room, the two discovered that an old phonograph in the corner of the large dining room was playing. Before deciding to stop it from playing, the young woman quickly went in search of her friend and owner of the house. As they entered the dining area, she asked him if he would mind if she turned the music off, as it was making it difficult to sleep. Confused, her friend explained that he had not started the music.

According to the owner, this was an old wind-up phonograph whose handle had to be cranked and turned several times over, then the needle placed on to the vinyl record, before it would even produce any type of sound. He assured them that he had not wound up the phonograph.

Together, the three walked over closer to the antique wooden box to inspect it. The music continued. The owner slowly and carefully lifted the lid to reveal that the record was indeed spinning around and around, with the needle in place as the warbled music continued to play. The owner lifted the needle from the record and moved the arm of the phonograph back to its resting place. He stopped the record gently with his fingers and in turn moved a little lever. The phonograph was now motionless. He closed the wooden lid, and the room was now silent. "It won't play now," said the owner with a smile, and with a few good-nights and a hug or two, they were once again off to bed.

As they all settled back in for the night, sleep was a welcomed companion.

About a quarter past three in the morning, the music could be heard again, but this time, it seemed to be playing a bit faster and louder than before.

The trio once again gathered in the dining room. They stood there looking at the phonograph, this time with the lid wide open. The phonograph was purposely playing, record spinning, needle down, and lid wide open, with no one visible to have cranked it!

It was decided that they would not make the music stop this time, but they would just let it play and go to their respective rooms for the night, with the only explanation being that of a ghostly occurrence—an unseen force that could actually manipulate the phonograph into filling the home with music. Apparently, there was a spirit there who wished to listen to the music and maybe even dance to the scratchy yet lovely notes. To this day, the owner cannot explain this incident, and it has not happened again.

BONJOUR!

Disembodied voices and whispers have also been heard within the walls of the Painted Lady. Small objects have been known to simply disappear and/or be relocated or just reappear within the home itself in another location.

Finally, after many odd things continued to happen in the Painted Lady, the owner decided to invite a paranormal investigation team into his home. He gave the team no information of the goings-on so they would have no prior knowledge; the owner just wanted to see what, if any, information could be obtained.

With a handheld voice recorder, an EVP (electronic voice phenomena) was recorded; it was of a conversation between two ladies who were apparently speaking in French. It was a short conversation, and the volume was faint. The exact specifics of the conversation could not be made out, but it was distinctly in the French language. "This would make sense," stated the current owner of the home, "as there is history of French Huguenots in this area." He also shared that the foldout windows on the second floor open onto the roof of the first floor. "They [the windows] have been known to open on their own, with no one being upstairs. It's as if someone opens the windows to walk out on a sunny day, maybe to enjoy the sunshine. I haven't seen her, but some insist that a young woman dressed in period clothing has also been seen by passersby, standing there, looking out of one of the top-floor windows, as if waiting and watching for someone."

EVPs of what sounds to be booted footsteps were also heard. Shadows were captured via digital photography. A voice of a very stern man was captured on the first floor.

Another incident that happened at this house that was not captured on film or EVP was that of a ghostly, transparent sighting of a black horse-drawn hearse (carriage) that was sitting directly in front of the house, with no explanation. It was as if it was there waiting; then it just disappeared. The gentleman that saw the carriage was unnerved and shaken and could not explain or understand why no one else could see it. He repeatedly stated that it was there, believing it could have been an omen of some sort.

Hidden spaces have been found in many places in the home, and the inside staircase that leads to the attic is most interesting and spooky; it is very narrow.

A mysterious key has been found in the home in one of the hidden spaces as well. The key does not fit in any of the doors, and to this day, no one knows just what the key unlocks or why it was hidden.

"This is also the house where two movie stars stayed while a Hollywood movie was being filmed in Abbeville," stated the owner. "They stayed in the top left-facing room, and that is where a lot of paranormal activity still seems to happen. When one is downstairs, footsteps and other noises of things sliding across the room can be heard."

According to a medium who has visited the home on many occasions, there is the spirit of a stern man who resides downstairs. "He is in a wheelchair, and he is a very egotistical, harsh man," stated the medium. "He says this is his house and it will always be his house." When the owner of the house heard this, he left the room and quickly returned with an old black-and-white photo of a large family. In that photo was a gentleman, apparently the patriarch of the group, sitting in his wheelchair with a stern look upon his face.

Above is a photo of the old stagecoach step in front of the historic Painted Lady home, where the horse-drawn hearse was seen in a ghostly image. There are a limited number of these left in America today. They were used as a step to get up into a stagecoach.

CHAPTER 7

Trinity Church and Cemetery

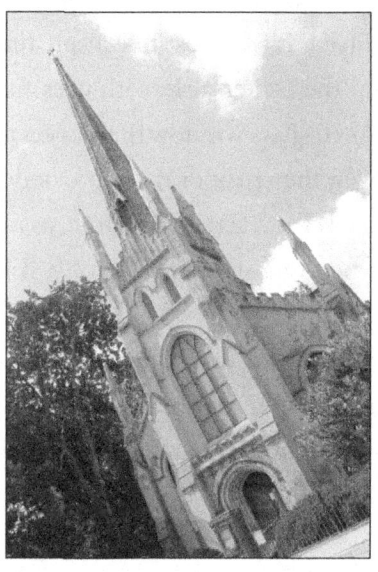

Trinity Episcopal Church is the oldest church building in the City of Abbeville and sits at the very end of Trinity Street. As one of the most visited historic landmarks in Abbeville, it is also one of the most majestic and beautifully designed churches in America. "Trinity," as it is referred to by locals, is also unique, as it is pink in color.

George Walker of Columbia was chosen as the designer of this Gothic-Revival-style cathedral. Although the building that stands today was built between the years of 1859 and 1860, the congregation itself began to gather for worship in 1842 in a frame building on the very same site. The original wooden church pews, as well as the large pipe organ built by John Baker in 1860, remain intact and in use today.

A sense of nostalgia is most evident when one enters the sanctuary itself. It is almost like a spiritual experience just to walk up the center aisle with eyes fixed upon the beautifully stained-glass window that serves as a backdrop to the altar. Even the creak of the old wooden floor adds character to the well-preserved building, as many have expressed that when one steps into Trinity, it is as if one is stepping back in time.

With a large majority of old, historic buildings, folklore and ghost stories emerge, and as you continue to read over the next few pages, you will see that Trinity is no different.

THE WEEPING LADY

My friend Susan and I had met in Abbeville to have supper with a few mutual friends. Yes, I said "supper"; to those of you who do not live in the South, "supper" is equivalent to "dinner." Anyway, we all enjoyed a lovely Mexican meal at one of our favorite corner restaurants in Abbeville called Maria's.

After we had all gotten our fill of delicious food, sweet tea, stories of days gone by, and laughter, we began to go our separate ways. Susan and I decided to take a walk around Abbeville for old times' sake. You see, Susan used to live in Abbeville, but she had since moved to the coast. Off we went on our walk down memory lane.

The sun had already hidden behind the buildings as we walked red brick roads that encircled the park in the middle of the town square. There were familiar store-fronts, along with new ones as well. Some faces that we passed we recognized; others were ones we had never seen before. Either way, with each passing, we were greeted with a friendly "hey," a wave, or a tip of a hat.

We then headed toward our favorite area located directly off to the side of the square. We were headed down Trinity Street.

Walking down the left side of Trinity Street, we passed a tall and wide wooden fence behind Maria's, a couple of empty buildings, the Grapevine Antique Store, another empty building, the old cloth shop, and an arcade on the farthest corner.

When we arrived at Trinity Episcopal Church, it had already closed for the day, but that did not matter to either of us. We just stood in adoration and admiration of the architectural masterpiece. It was as if we were looking upon a medieval castle. I felt like a tiny person as I gazed upon the majestic towers. We both stood in silent awe and relished the moment as we always had when we visited this building. Both of us had expressed to each other on many occasions that Trinity has always been and will always remain one of our favorite places to visit.

After a few moments of nostalgia, I reached for my cell phone to take a photo. While doing so, I explained to Susan that on one occasion when I visited the church, I heard a woman weeping. As I followed the sound of her cries, they turned into wails, and I began to call 911 on my cell phone because I just knew someone needed help. But as I kept walking, the cries had now turned into screams of "No! No! Noooooo!" Then, before me, I saw a transparent lady who had a white glow about her. She was wearing a long, dark, period dress and was sitting on the ground hugging what I thought was a baby, but the closer I got, I saw it was a soldier's uniform with which she was wiping her tears. I stood motionless and silent. I did not know whether to try to comfort her or run, but running was not an option because I felt as if I didn't even have a physical body. I was frozen, as frozen as a cement statue. I couldn't move even if I had tried. I wanted to scream for help, but no sound would come out. I wanted to dial 911, but my phone was no longer in my hand. I must have dropped it.

I closed my eyes, trying to convince myself that I was not seeing what I thought I saw. I took a deep breath and then opened my eyes. The weeping had subsided. The woman was no longer there. She was gone. She had seemed to suddenly...disappear! Confused and dazed, I looked down and saw that my phone was lying on the road beside me. I looked around to see if there was anyone else who may have seen or heard the weeping woman. There was no one. I hurriedly walked to my car and sat there for a moment to compose myself.

As I finished telling of my ghostly experience, I pointed the exact spot out to Susan where I'd seen the weeping lady. Oddly, there was a bare spot in the grass; it was just dirt there, no vegetation. "It was near a tree. I remember distinctly that she was sitting near *that* tree!" I said as I pointed again and began to tear up.

We headed back up Trinity Street, as it was now beginning to get really dark and there was no one left on the street but us two.

"Oh my," said Susan when we were halfway up the street. "That's so sad." As she reached to place her hand on my shoulder to comfort me, at that exact moment, we both heard a scream of a woman, followed by weeping. The cries were coming from behind us at the church! We were startled, and the chills in our bodies told us it was time to leave. The cries only lasted for a few seconds, and by now, the only light was that of a few streetlights. We did not go back. We kicked it in high gear and jumped in our cars, locked our doors, and waved goodbye.

To this day, I have neither seen nor heard the weeping woman again, and I have visited the church many more times. But similar stories are told by others of the weeping lady.

As I was sharing my story with a local historian, I was told that the spirit of a woman by the name of Elizabeth Mitchell reputedly haunts the grounds of Trinity Church. Supposedly, her husband was killed while fighting in a war, and to this day, she mourns him. Others say Elizabeth's young child was killed and that is why she weeps; either way, the cries that are heard are those of one mourning the loss of a loved one.

On one particular occasion, a young girl was in the church with her mother, and the young girl was talking to someone who, apparently, could only be seen by her! The mother did not see anyone there and asked her daughter who she was talking to, as they were the only two people in the church. The young girl turned to her mother with a smile and said, "Her name is Elizabeth."

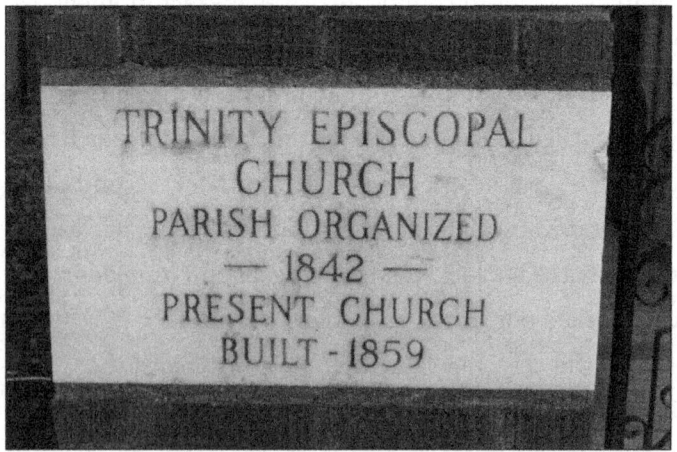

THE TRINITY CEMETERY

The cemetery of Trinity Episcopal Church is located several hundred feet behind the church, and it cannot be seen from the front or the back of the church itself. It can only be accessed via a road that runs to the left behind the church and from a neighboring street on the right.

Established in 1852, Trinity is the oldest known cemetery in the City of Abbeville, although there are older cemeteries in Abbeville County. The first burial here was that of a young child, and the last burial was in the year 1980.

It is said that the eighteen Confederate soldiers who were laid to rest here cannot rest peacefully, as there is one Union soldier buried among them. Several photos have been taken of what appears to be young men in their uniforms at this graveyard. It is as if they are guarding the cemetery, as they all seem to be armed in the photos.

The story of the one and only Union soldier who is buried at Trinity Cemetery is quite unique. He was originally from New York, where he was a dock worker. The war had ended, and he had been sent to Abbeville from Charleston to help move a unit of soldiers. He was also asked to protect a local family for the night after an altercation between one of their family members and a soldier who was scheduled to leave the next day. A gunshot was heard as the family enjoyed dinner that evening, and when the Union soldier ran through the hall of their home to investigate, another shot was heard. This bullet struck the guardian in the head, and he instantly fell to the floor and to his death.

The Union soldier's funeral was said to be most beautiful, as the ladies of Abbeville filled the church with local flowers in bloom from their gardens. The nameless soldier was buried and seemingly forgotten. The only identification marking the grave: "the Yankee soldier."

However, this ghost does not haunt or linger in this cemetery. He is said to inhabit a home in the City of Abbeville, still protecting the family members who live there present-day. His ghostly image can be seen standing on the front porch of the home he was protecting. Apparently, this soldier has no idea he is dead. Over a hundred years passed before someone researched his life and then placed his name upon his grave marker—Peter Hanley, 1834–1865.

Buried also in this cemetery are the remains of church members, soldiers, generals, and their family members.

Many apparitions have been captured in photos at this cemetery, and many ghostly goings-on have been experienced and recorded. Giggles of children playing, phantom musket-shot sounds, smells of gunpowder, and the unexplained fragrance of ladies' perfume that often lingers in the air are all examples of haunted happenings at Trinity Cemetery. Conversations have also been heard between several people when no one can visibly be seen.

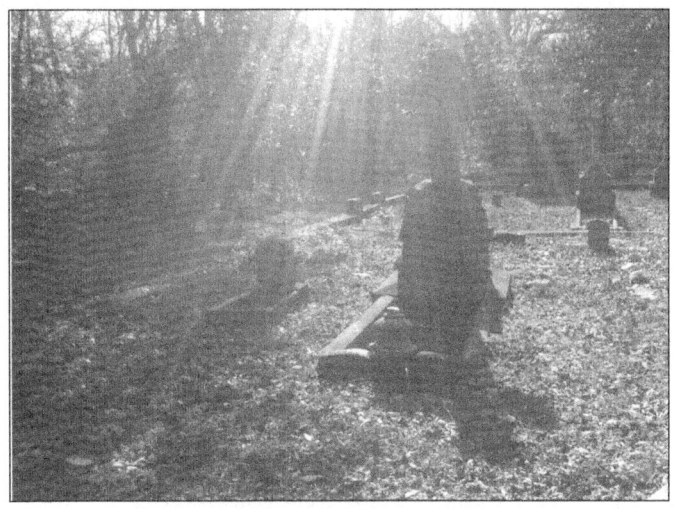

How many apparitions can you spot in this photo that was taken at Trinity Cemetery? Look closely! There is a man on a horse, a crying child, and a few others.

CHAPTER 8

The Ghost of the Radio Station

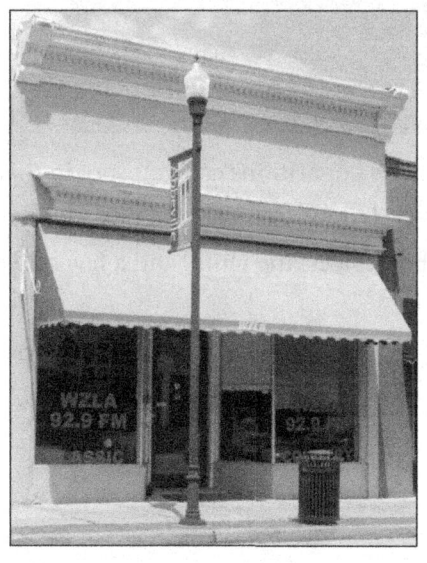

WZLA is the local radio station in Abbeville, the office of which is located in a building on Main Street. Classic country music is the station's genre, but there's more to the building the station calls home than just the sound of music.

According to morning radio hosts and radio personalities Benji Greeson, Amy Botts, and Lacey Yates, strange things happen both when they are on air and when they are not.

One incident that occurred was that of a door moving on its own accord. "I heard something that sounded like something was being dragged or slid across the floor, so I went to the back to see what it was. *The door was actually open!*" exclaimed Greeson, his eyes growing wide. "There was stuff in front of the door and even paper on the floor that was pushed away, and *there was no one there!* There was *no way* that that door could have opened on its own." He laughed nervously. "But it did!" Greeson continued to explain that the door was locked and opened from the inside and that this incident cannot, to this day, be logically explained.

Another occurrence that happened was in June of 2017. A radio guest saw a tall, thin, transparent gentleman walking through the radio station. As he was walking, he was humming and whistling a happy tune. He reportedly walked all the way to the back of the station and disappeared into the back wall, never to be seen again.

Other mysterious sounds and strange goings-on have been witnessed; objects moving and being dropped have also been reported.

"Well, I can't say exactly *what* I heard, but there have been many times that I've heard things and felt like I wasn't alone in here," added Botts.

Greeson shared yet another creepy event that happened just a few months later in August of 2017. "Well, I just watched a pair of scissors move six or eight inches inside of a container on my desk—out of the blue. No rhyme or reason to it! The scissors were on the right side of the container. It [the container] *did not* fall," insisted Greeson. "The scissors slowly slid to another position, which they are in now. Geesh…that was freaky! When it happened, I went kinda cold, like I knew it was somebody trying to get my attention." Greeson insisted he was simply sitting still at his desk, and as he was reading and reviewing football notes, this hauntingly eerie incident occurred.

The newest addition to the radio family is radio personality Lacey Yates. "Yeah, I've seen and felt some weird things in this building since I have been here," she said. "There is no doubt that there is something in there! I hear footsteps a lot when there is nobody else in the building. There's a door in there that opens and shuts by itself as well. To me, the back of the building is creepier than the front. Lots of strange things have been happening. There is no doubt that I am never alone in this building—even when I am by myself."

CHAPTER 9
The Old Jail and Museum

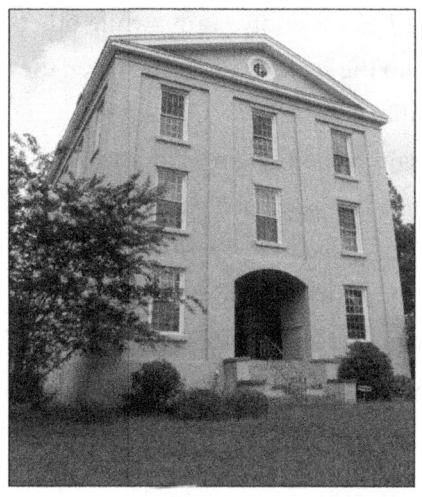

In 1854, Abbeville's oldest public building was built, the Old Jail, designed by none other than Robert Mills, the architect who famously designed the Washington Monument.

The building is three stories tall, and the top floor was built to house the most hardened and dangerous criminals, constructed with large, high beams that served as a perfect hanging spot. The middle floor would hold the not-so-violent prisoners, and the bottom floor would serve as a home for the sheriff.

The Old Jail is located on the corner of Henry M. Turner and Poplar Streets, and now serves as the county museum.

EARL

Some say Earl is a friendly entity, while others claim that Earl gave them the scare of a lifetime when they visited the Old Jail in Abbeville.

Earl is said to be the ghost of an African-American male between the ages of twenty-five and thirty, who was accused of murder and refuses to leave the top floor of the jail. Some stories claim that Earl was hanged for his crime from the large rafters on the third floor, while others insist he died of natural causes while serving his time. Regardless, Earl has decided that he will never leave.

On one occasion, a visitor to the museum went up to the third floor to see the displays. This visitor heard a deep laugh and the words "get out" in her right ear. Needless to say, that visitor left, never to return.

Another patron claims a chair abruptly fell over like it had been kicked (just as a chair would be kicked out from underneath someone who was being hanged). Some prisoners may have hanged themselves; others were hanged by cellmates; and others yet hanged by the sheriff for their crimes.

Some have claimed that Earl has been nothing but kind and mannerly to them. One such incident was when Earl seemed distraught, as he thought people were coming to throw him out of his home and he wanted to stay there in the Old Jail. He was relieved to know he was welcome to stay.

The artwork in this historic building is very interesting, especially on the top floor. A blackbird was drawn on the wall and is believed to be the artwork of one of the prisoners incarcerated in the past. The blackbird is known to be an ominous symbol of death in some cultures, and many believe that is why one of the prisoners drew it on the wall.

A past curator of the museum claims he could hear what sounded like footsteps on the top two floors when he was down on the first level. He also reported that on many occasions it sounded like furniture was being moved or dragged across the floor. Scratches were also heard within the walls. Displays in the museum would be moved about during the night, only to be put back into place by the curator the next morning.

The ghost of Earl has reportedly been seen in the top window of the building during a full moon. According to many here in Abbeville, his name is Earl Miller and he has been in the old jail building since 1905—and has no intentions of leaving.

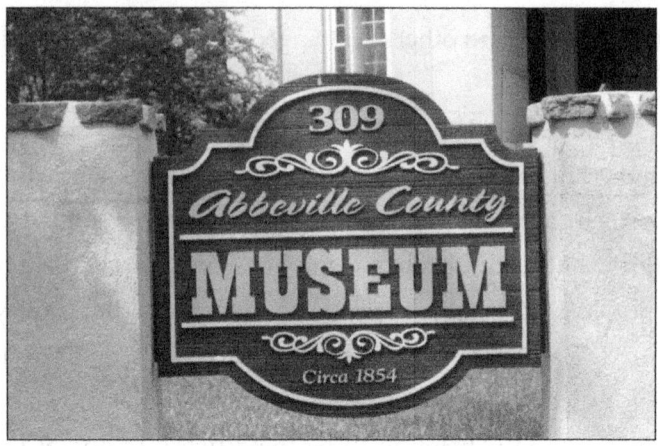

There is another area behind and underneath the Abbeville County Courthouse made up of a few jail cells that is also very spiritually active. There are video and audio recordings of ghostly activity. This area has not been utilized for decades, but the bunks and steel jail cell doors, although weathered, are still in place.

CHAPTER 10

Spirits on the Square

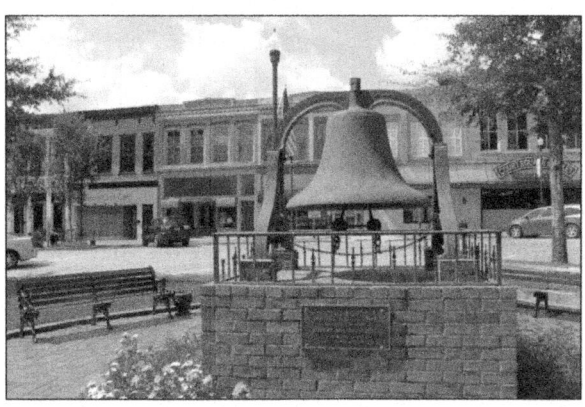

The square is the busiest hub in Abbeville County. From live theatre to specialty restaurants, from a marketplace to a livery stable, from a moonshine distillery to unique specialty clothing stores, the square has something for everyone. "Big Bob" is the large iron warning bell that has been there for over a hundred years and was erected in the late 1890s in honor of Mayor Robert McGowan Hill.

The square is also home to a monument that marks historical significance. Large, majestic trees, whose roots run as deep as its history, adorn the center of the quaint Southern town.

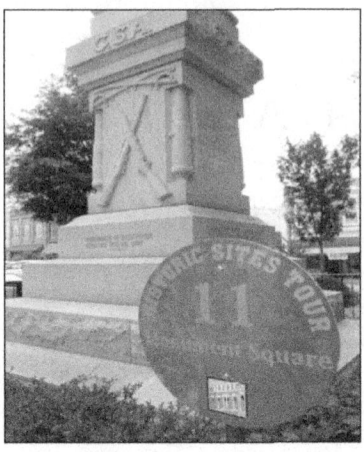

A green space, now a park, is a sought-after destination. With that said, the square, too, has its share of mysterious and spooky activity.

MEET "MISS PENNY"

If ever you decide to take a walk around the square in Abbeville, you might just encounter the happy spirit of Miss Penny.

Miss Penny is the spirit of a little old lady who is of African descent. Her skin is flawless and smooth except for the hundreds of wrinkles that show when she smiles, which is almost always. Her smile consists of only a few teeth, and her gray eyes always have a twinkle.

Penny carries a small, black leather change purse that fits in the palm of her hand. The purse has two compartments that are kept closed by a silver metal twist as the clasp. Penny has only been seen walking in front of the old bank building, wearing clothing from what appears to be from the 1970s, along with her yellow pillbox hat and white gloves.

Penny has been known to approach people and only utter, "My name is Penny," before she then simply vanishes into the bank building's door.

THE BLACK STALLION

Many people who have entered the historic livery stable have shared that they smell the aroma of horses, hay, and feed, which wouldn't normally be unusual—except the building hasn't housed horses for several decades now.

Some people claimed they not only smelled but *saw* horses in the livery stable. There is one particular horse that many people have claimed to see not only in the livery stable, but in and around town. He is a massive black horse with a well-groomed, long mane and tail—a muscular horse of impeccable breeding. His coat is so black that it has a blue glow to it when the streetlight shines upon it.

This translucent stallion has also reputedly been seen trotting around the square, seemingly with no destination, just a slow prance throughout the streets. He has even reportedly been seen on the grounds of the nearby Trinity Church Cemetery, near the graves of soldiers and generals. Some believe that perhaps this noble steed is in search of his fallen master among the graves.

THE TROUGH/FOUNTAIN

Little translucent figures believed to resemble little dogs, and maybe even cats, have been seen in and around this antique turn-of-the-century water fountain.

Some of these ghostly figures rush by people or rub up against them. Others seem to only be seen by children who laugh and giggle playfully with them in or near the water.

This five-ton masterpiece was ingenious in its time and was gifted to Abbeville in 1912 as a humane effort to ensure workhorses and other animals had water. It is known as a watering trough/fountain and has two decks of different heights: the tall deck, for horses, and the lower tier, with small bowls for domesticated animals such as dogs and cats.

This fountain still sits in its original location, which is most rare. Only 125 of these humane gestures were granted across the United States by the National Humane Alliance.

An informational marker has been placed in front of the old yellow bank building on Main Street near the fountain.

THE ROUGH HOUSE

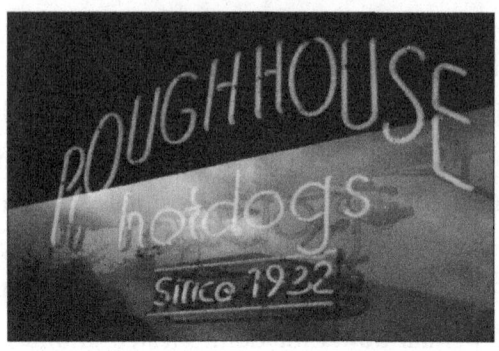

Known most popularly for its famous hot dogs and "Q-dogs" (barbecue on a hot dog bun), the Rough House of Abbeville has its own share of haunted happenings.

"I would be down here serving customers in the restaurant and hear footsteps coming from upstairs on the second floor, knowing good and well there was nobody up there," said Shelley Reid, the former owner of the restaurant. "I just couldn't explain it. I know there was no one up there because that's where I live!"

The Rough House is also a popular meeting place for paranormal groups from all over the southeast. On several occasions, two nationally recognized producers and directors have filmed paranormal segments in and around the establishment.

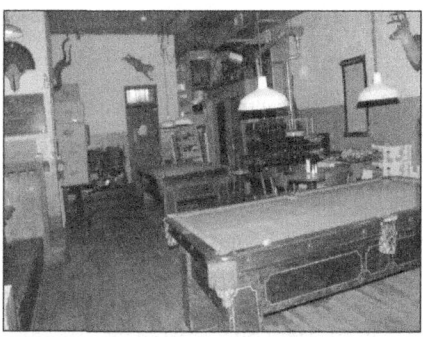

Several paranormal teams have also conducted investigations and obtained numerous disembodied voices and phantom footprints.

WHISTLE WHILE YOU WORK

The old bank building was built in the mid-1800s and can today easily be spotted on the square in the downtown area. The building is painted bright yellow and trimmed in black. Located at 107 Court Square, there is reportedly a busy spirit who dwells within its walls.

"He's an older man, and we can hear him whistling all the time," shared a former volunteer for the Abbeville Chamber of Commerce, the offices of which currently occupy the building. "A medium visited us one day several years ago and described the man as an older white man around sixty or seventy years old. She said he was wearing blue jean overalls and a white short-sleeved t-shirt. Each time he was seen, he was apparently sweeping or mopping the floor of the bank, so we were okay with that," she joked.

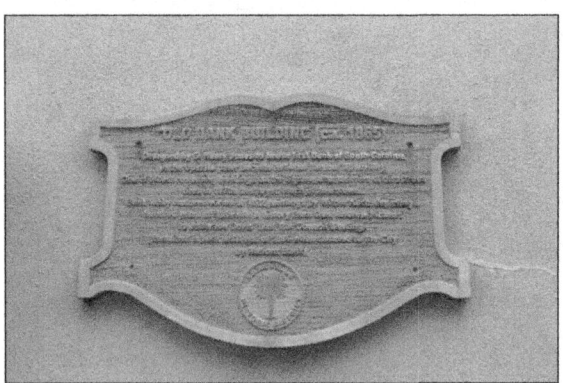

This spirit is believed to be a content apparition, as he can be heard—even when he can't be seen—whistling while he works.

THE LADY OF MARIA'S

Maria's is one of the most popular eating establishments in Abbeville. Located on the corner of Court Square and Trinity Street, this restaurant has a friendly ghost who is most fond of male patrons.

With distinctly dark, raven hair, this spirit is described as wearing a long skirt but dressed most provocatively from the waist up. She has reportedly been seen in the far right-facing window on the second floor.

"She seems to be looking out over the square and waiting on someone," said a patron of the establishment. "I have also seen her face in the mirror in the upstairs bathroom."

She seems to particularly make herself visible to male patrons dining in the upstairs area. Some who have witnessed her manifestation believe she may have even been a lady of the evening. One gentleman said he had never believed in ghosts before, but while he was eating in the upstairs bar area, he heard a woman's voice whisper, "Hello, soldier." He said he also felt someone caressing his hair a few moments later.

This lady ghost also seems to be very jealous. One evening when a group of friends had gathered for an evening meal, one of the women in the group went to the bathroom to wash her hands. As she turned to leave the restroom, she could not seem to get the door open. When someone finally helped her out, she headed back to her table to sit beside her husband. As she approached her chair, she saw this beautiful transparent woman sitting in her chair beside her husband. No one else at the table saw the ghostly figure. The women pulled the chair out, and the figure disappeared. After the lady sat down, her glass of water fell over and spilled all over her. The woman ordered another glass of water, which then also tipped over and covered her with ice and water.

This promiscuous lady is often seen standing at the top of the stairs. Can you see her in the following photo?

CHAPTER 11

The Livery Stable

Originally constructed in the early 1820s, the livery stable of Abbeville was used for the sole purpose of a stable. Located on Trinity Street, this stable was later (in the early twentieth century) converted into a wholesale business by Mr. W.G. Bowie, which it remained for most of that century. After the wholesale business closed, the Bowie family donated the building to the City of Abbeville. It sat empty for many years.

In the early 2000s, two South Carolina National Heritage Corridor grants were received, and with their help, the livery stable was not only saved but restored and converted into a public space. It is open daily and can be reserved for public and/or private events. Open markets, wedding receptions, parties, and other private and public gatherings are held there.

MYSTERIOUS ORBS

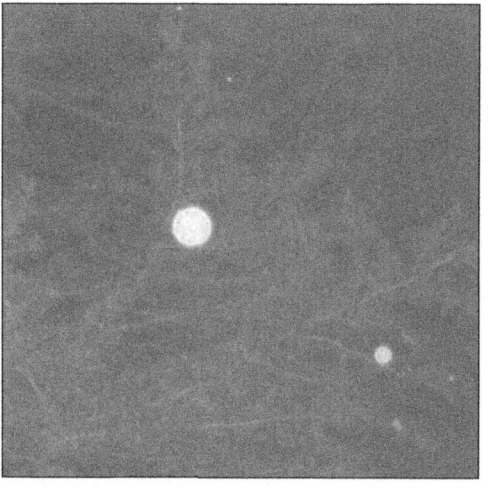

Being that the old livery stable is now a venue for many different types of events, thousands upon thousands of photographs are taken there each year. In many of these photographs, strange orbs appear. Yes, while some people believe that these little circles of light are merely particles of dust, others say they are drops of condensation from the evening dew. Light bulbs that are turned on, flickering flames from candles that are lit, and even flashes from a camera can also create such circles of reflection in the air. It could even be a little bug or gnat flying about when a picture is being taken! There are so many possibilities and ways to debunk the story of a small circle of light that is referred to as an "orb."

However, in the paranormal world, many people believe and define a small percentage of these small round orbs as "spirit balls," which seem to have their own source of light. Many of these intriguing spheres have been captured in photographs and on video recordings. Some are clear and transparent, while others are vivid and colorful. Some people have claimed to see actual faces within these free-floating circles after zooming in on photographs.

Dust, when stirred up, can fly around in sporadic patterns, yet gravity ultimately settles the dust in a downward motion. Orbs, on the other hand, have their own flight pattern, sometimes continuing to rise and float to what seems to be their own purposeful destination.

You may want to look back at your own photos that have been taken in or around the Abbeville Livery Stable. Who knows? You may have unknowingly captured the face of a wandering spirit in its own little "ghost bubble."

CHAPTER 12

The Burt-Stark Mansion

Located at the triangular point of North Main Street in Abbeville, the Burt-Stark Mansion may be the most well-known historic landmark and home in Abbeville. This two-story architectural jewel is also known as the Armistead Burt House (after Confederate Major Armistead Burt, who once resided in the home). This beautiful and large mansion is also the reason Abbeville itself is known as the "Deathbed of the Confederacy." In the front parlor of this lovely home is where Confederate President Jefferson Davis signed the papers to end the Civil War.

This Greek-Revival home was built in the 1830s by David Lesley, a lawyer, district judge, and planter. Judge Lesley lived there with his family until his death in 1855. Since then, there have been six other owners.

From 1855 to 1859, it was owned by a Presbyterian pastor by the name of Thomas A. Hoyt; from 1859 to 1862, it was owned by a banker from Charleston, South Carolina, Andrew Simonds.

Between1862 and 1868, it was owned by Major Armistead Burt, who owned it when Jefferson Davis ended the Civil War. After the fall of the war, Burt was forced to sell the mansion because he went bankrupt.

James R. Norwood, a local planter, purchased the home from Burt in 1868. Norwood then died in 1875, and his widow and daughter inherited the home and owned it until 1900, when James Samuel Stark purchased it from the Norwood family. Stark's daughter, Mary Stark Davis, ultimately inherited the home, and she was the last known relative to reside in the historic home.

"Miss Mary" took pride in caring for the home and in keeping its heritage alive. She passed away in 1987 and had already donated the home and its contents to the Abbeville Historic Preservation Commission, who owns and maintains the mansion presently.

Entering the home, the antique furniture and décor seems to transport visitors back in time; the feeling of nostalgia seems to engulf all who enter. Many tourists have reported feeling "chills," "goose bumps," or just plain "eerie feelings" as they enter the home. The atmosphere has been described by many as "electric." There are reports of many unexplained goings-on in this house, events and ghostly happenings that to date cannot logically or scientifically be explained. What follows is just a few of the ghostly stories that have been shared over the years.

A LOYAL SOLDIER

The front bedroom on the right-facing corner is the room where Confederate President Jefferson Davis stayed the night he visited. Stories of seeing the ghost of a Confederate soldier have been reported many times over the last decade, in this room and only in this room. Some believe it is the ghost of a loyal Confederate soldier still keeping watch over President Davis. Others who have seen this apparition believe it is the spirit of Jefferson Davis himself in his dress uniform. Reports of a man clearing his throat have reportedly been heard and captured via EVP.

MISS MARY

"Miss Mary" has also been seen in the mansion. However, her ghostly yet friendly figure has been seen by many in almost every room in the house!

"She still takes care of the house and looks over it," stated one member of the Abbeville Historical Society, who wished to remain anonymous. "Mary," she continued, "was the last known relative to own the house. In 1970, the home was listed in the National Register, and in October of 1982, it was designated as a National Historic Landmark. Miss Mary would have been so proud!"

THE WHISTLING SERVANT

In the days of old, when servants would cook the meals for the privileged and upper class, many of the home's kitchens were separated from the main house. Such is the case in this mansion. As a documentary was being filmed on the grounds of the Burt-Stark Mansion, whistling could be heard continuously and was even captured on audio equipment. No one could figure it out until the tour guide explained, "Decades ago, when the servants would cook in the detached kitchen, the owners of the home would make the servants whistle all the way from the kitchen to the main house. This would ensure that the servants were not eating the food between the kitchen and the main house."

THE LOVELY LADY

There are several reports of a full-bodied apparition of a lovely Southern lady seen at this historic home, descending the tall staircase in the mansion. No one seems to know the story or reasoning behind this ghostly figure. She is a most primly dressed young woman with a tiny silhouette. This "Southern belle" has also been unexpectedly caught on film, as well as in digital photos of the home.

CHAPTER 13

Raventap

Raventap Restaurant and Pub (formerly known as Natty's) is located on the infamous Trinity Street, which is adjacent to Main Street in Abbeville. Strange things happen on a regular basis in this restaurant-style eclectic bar.

"Well, we've had a lot of weird things happen here," explains owner Judson Arce with a slight smile, eyebrows raised. "Everything from glasses moving across the bar to shadowy figures being seen; but most often, the basement door will open on its own." Arce explained that there are tunnels underneath the streets of downtown Abbeville that were utilized hundreds of years ago. "Perhaps whoever visits us here at Raventap [from the spirit world], well, they might just be looking for a way out, trying to get to those tunnels! There's no telling how many people may have gotten trapped in the tunnels and died. There may even be spirits residing within the tunnel walls. It's not certain if the tunnels were used to transport goods or if they were an escape route for people who were trying to flee for their safety, possibly from native attacks. Abbeville has so many historical events, there's no telling," concluded Arce. "But one thing is for sure: our basement door opens and shuts on its own, and we are a very spiritually active location!"

There are several more ghostly happenings that have occurred at Raventap, including footprints on the top floor that were heard when no one was up there; a lady in a long period dress on the stairs leading to the landing above; a phantom smell of horse feed and hay; people sitting at the bar who have been tapped on the shoulder and there's no one there when they turn around.

CHAPTER 14

The Restless Mob

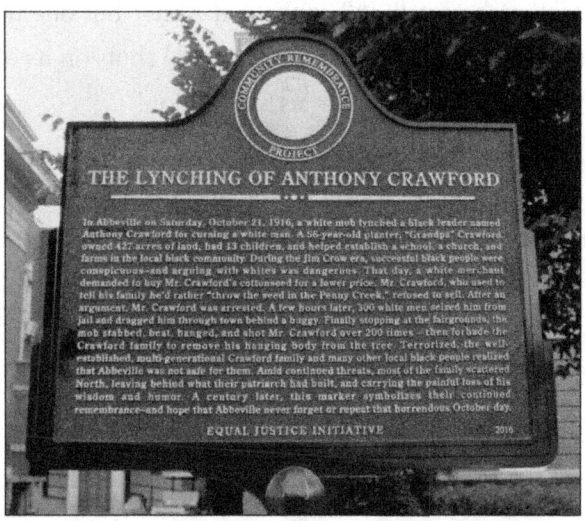

During the early 1900s, there was a lot of racial tension in the entire South, from which Abbeville County was not excluded. With that said, the lynching of Anthony Crawford cannot go unmentioned. "Grandpa Crawford," as he is known to many, owned 427 acres in the Abbeville area, which was almost unheard of in the early 1900s for a black man. This hard-working father of thirteen children farmed cotton.

In October of 1916, a white merchant reportedly demanded to pay Crawford less than what he was asking for his crop. Crawford allegedly refused to sell at the low price and, in turn, cursed the white merchant. It is written in history that Crawford was not only arrested, but a mob of white men took Crawford from the jail and dragged him behind a buggy all the way through town, beating and stabbing him repeatedly. They ultimately hanged him and shot his hanging corpse over two hundred times. The family of Crawford was reportedly forbidden to take down his body and, in fear of their own lives, eventually fled north.

Known to many as a leader who did great things, Anthony Crawford is credited with such wonderful things as having established a church, school, and several productive farms in order to better the lives of not only the black community, but the entire Abbeville community.

One might think that dying such an unjust and horrendous death, Anthony Crawford himself might haunt the streets of Abbeville, but strangely enough, Crawford seems to be resting in eternal peace—while it seems his attackers are the souls who wander. Ghostly figures of some of these men seem lost, while others seem still angry; either way, they are indeed restless souls.

Visitors, tourists, and residents alike have reportedly seen male figures wandering about town, near the courthouse, and even near the fairgrounds outside of town where Crawford was eventually hanged.

A marker has been erected near the Abbeville Courthouse by the Equal Justice Initiative in hopes that a lynching such as this will never happen again.

CHAPTER 15

The Quay-Wardlaw House

The Quay-Wardlaw House (pronounced "Key-Wardlaw") is the oldest recorded standing building in the City of Abbeville. Built in 1786 around an original log cabin, it is a very ghostly property.

Previous owners of this homestead encountered several different spirits. Children of the home have reportedly seen an elderly couple dressed in period clothing. Family pets have appeared to be watching someone cross the room when no one can be seen. Silverware goes missing and is found in odd places in the house, even on the top floor! Unknown figures have been seen in the upstairs dormer windows, especially on nights there is a full moon.

It has been told that the ghosts who inhabit this home do not like for anyone to stand in front of the original fireplace, which is located in the original log cabin portion of the home. This seems to be not only the heart of the home, but the dwelling place of much spiritual activity.

Children's clothes have also been mysteriously removed from a closet in the home, and strangely, head pillows are often taken and placed *underneath* the bed!

The aroma of roses can be smelled in the home at times, and cool drafts have reportedly been felt on a regular basis.

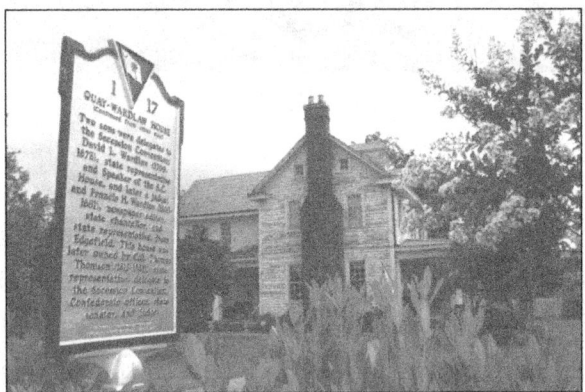

AUTHOR'S NOTE

Thank you for reading. One may understand now why Abbeville, South Carolina, can be deemed one of the most haunted areas not only in South Carolina or the southeast, but the entire nation!

Readers of *The Apparitions of Abbeville: The History & Mystery of the South Carolina Lakelands* may also be interested in the first book of this series, *Ghost Stories of Uptown Greenwood*, available on Amazon and Kindle.

To schedule speaking engagements or book-signing events with Marjorie LaNelle, you may contact her via email: marjorielanelle@yahoo.com.

Made in the USA
Columbia, SC
26 August 2023

22071885R00075